Tradition and Folk Life

Tradition and Folk Life

A Welsh View

by

IORWERTH C. PEATE

FABER AND FABER LTD
3 Queen Square, London

First published in 1972
by Faber and Faber Limited
3 Queen Square, London WC1
Printed in Great Britain
by W & J Mackay Limited, Chatham

ISBN 0 571 09804 5

I'm cyfaill
SÉAMUS Ó DUILEARGA
'Llawn o ddiddanwch . . . a haelaf ei fron'
ac i gofio cyfaill arall
ÅKE CAMPBELL
'. . . dewr hyd ddiwedd y daith'

Contents

List of Illustrations

Unless otherwise acknowledged, the copyright of all the illustrations is that of the National Museum of Wales (Welsh Folk Museum). Plates 5, 13, 53, 54 and 55 are from photographs by the author.

Preface

This book is not a textbook for students of Folk Life. It has been written at the request of several persistent friends who have thought that, after a professional life of well over forty years, I would have something of value to say about some aspects of a vast subject. I trust that they will not be disappointed.

I am grateful to the authorities of the National Museum of Wales (Welsh Folk Museum) for allowing me to use many of the photographs in the Welsh Folk Museum collection to illustrate the volume; to several of my former colleagues for suggestions and, in particular, to Mr D. Roy Saer for reading the draft of Chapter 6; to Miss M. H. Judd and Mrs Mary Brown for preparing the typescript; and to my friend and fellow-countryman, Mr George Ewart Evans, for constant advice and many useful suggestions.

March, 1971 I.C.P.

Introduction

When I first entered the museum profession early in 1927, the term 'folk life' was not in use. There was, in the Department of Archaeology in the National Museum of Wales, a small but representative collection of what were called 'Welsh Bygones'. Such collections were, and are still, to be found in many museums. They were looked upon as appendages to the study of archaeology and when in 1932 we were successful in instituting a sub-department of 'Folk Culture and Industries' (the first of its kind in the United Kingdom), this too was within the department of Archaeology. It was laid down that the sub-department was concerned only with material of the post-1536 period; this date was chosen because, as the date of the Act of Union of Wales with England, it defined for practical museum purposes the end of the medieval period. That is, the study of 'bygones' was not considered to be within the field of medieval, Dark Ages, Roman or prehistoric archaeology, but merely a post-medieval appendage to it. When in 1936, a full Department of Folk Life was instituted—the term 'folk life' was now given official sanction—these limitations still remained.

I have discussed in another place[1] the importance of folk studies in museums. Archaeology does not end in one year and folk life begin in the next. To differentiate between the two fields of study, the chronological criterion cannot be accepted. Folk Life cannot be considered as a mere tail-piece to the study of archaeology. Folk Life is the study of man's material, mental and spiritual struggle towards civilization; that struggle did not begin at the end of the Middle Ages.

The methods of the archaeologist and the folk-life student are dissimilar. In archaeology, excavation with its attendant problems of scientific deduction based upon stratigraphy etc. is the main basis. Archaeology is that aspect of the study of mankind which depends

[1] Iorwerth C. Peate: 'The place of folk culture in the Museum', in *Museums Journal*, 41, 1941, pp. 45–50.

ultimately upon spade and pick. This is the archaeological method and it can be applied to the exploration of monuments of the historic as well as to the prehistoric period, to the excavation of a Norman castle or a medieval abbey, a Dark Ages site or a nineteenth-century industrial ruin. Fundamentally, the whole structure of archaeology is built on this foundation.

Much of what the archaeologist discovers is of importance to the student of folk life. In the reconstruction of a primitive culture, all that the archaeologist can provide are 'a few decayed objects of iron, a few potsherds, a stone quern and some beads'.[1] But they may be remnants of a complex culture which included wooden huts, woven grasswork, rush mats, skins or textile clothing, grass ropes, sinew string and wooden dishes. Any reconstruction of such a culture uninformed by a knowledge of folk life would be indeed (to quote Randall MacIver's well-known dictum) 'blind of one eye and very short-sighted of the other'.

The study of folk life is that of man's mental, spiritual and material struggle towards civilization; of 'that complex whole' (to quote E. B. Tylor[2]) 'which includes knowledge, belief, art, morals, law, custom and any other capabilities and habits acquired by man as a member of society'. It is a study of man in relation to his past and to his environment. Tylor[3] in his day, bid us 'look at the modern European peasant using his hatchet and his hoe, see his food boiling or roasting over the log fire, observe the exact place which beer holds in his calculation of happiness, hear his tale of the farmer's niece who was bewitched with knots in her inside till she fell into fits and died. If we choose out in this way things which have altered little in a long course of centuries, we may draw a picture where there shall be scarce a hand's breadth difference between an English ploughman and a negro of central Africa'. Undoubtedly there is a sense in which all mankind is one, but local conditions of life, the response to different environments and the spread of that 'blanket of sameness' created from the warp of industry and the weft of technology—those two 'blessed' words of the mid-twentieth

[1] R. U. Sayce: *Primitive Arts and Crafts*, Cambridge, 1933, p. 9.
[2] E. B. Tylor: *Primitive Culture*, I, London, 1929, p. 235.
[3] ibid.

century—have changed Tylor's world. There are gradations in culture and while one may still set some of man's traditional practices and beliefs side by side, whether they be on the Atlantic fringe of Europe, in London or Cairo or Moscow or Tokyo or Buenos Aires or the deserts of Africa or Asia, there are many senses in which Dr. Johnson's contemptuous dictum that 'one set of savages is like another' is completely false. Time and place change many things, and Tylor would find it difficult to recognize his 'English Ploughman' today. Tradition and a changing environment—these are factors of inestimable importance in the life of man. Neither one should be isolated at the expense of the other. 'Anthropologists,' stated a recent Malinowski Memorial lecturer,[1] 'no less than the people they study, are much given to the elaboration of those traditions by which men everywhere seek to justify their current interests and activities in terms of some mystically hallowed past.' This is fair comment, but tradition links each man with his past and part of the duty of the student of folk life is to interpret the role of tradition in our lives.

A simple example can be given from the field of material culture. One of the fashionable hearth implements of the seventeenth and eighteenth centuries was the lever-operated pot-crane (Plate 1). To lift the suspended pot from the fire the lever was depressed and held under one of the several knobs on the face of the crane: a reverse movement lowered it. In the first half of the nineteenth century, a Llangollen smith made a pot-crane now in the Welsh Folk Museum (Plate 2). This was the simple type without lever action but the lever knobs appear on it as ornamentation. Their only purpose was a decorative one: indeed, it is quite possible, even likely, that the smith was unaware that they were relics of a strictly functional feature now surviving as decoration. The buttons on the sleeves of men's jackets are a similar instance. In the same way tradition retains in the social order fashions, beliefs and institutions long after their prime usefulness has departed—the pageantry of the state openings of Parliament and, as some would maintain, even national sovereignty itself.

[1] I. M. Lewis in *Man: the Journal of the Royal Anthropological Institute*, London, 1966, p. 107.

Material culture and the role of tradition in its formation loom large in the study of folk life. But they are not the only part of the discipline. We are much concerned also with the spirit and mind of man. As the late Sigurd Erixon once declared (somewhat ponderously, perhaps): 'the products of man's physical actions are indications of the co-operation between his physiological and spiritual energies'.[1] But man's ideas—about life, death and immortality, for instance—are products of his mind and spirit only. Throughout the ages, men's ideas about such fundamental themes have remained: some greatly developed, others almost unchanged. Probably the oldest of them all is the concept of Love which arose from the long physical and emotional relationship between the human mother and her child. This relationship, as several distinguished anthropologists (e.g. the late H. J. Fleure and R. R. Marrett) have shown, is a fundamental principle in all mammalian life. But it is only in man, particularly because of the length of the relationship between the human mother and her child, in contrast with most other mammals, that Love developed into an important social energy. It attained the perfection of its flowering in the life and teaching of Jesus of Nazareth. The personal belief of the human father in Justice developed into social importance in various juridical systems, with the influence of the Grace and Mercy of religion evident in several of them. The ideas of our ancient forebears concerning life and death, preserved for us in folk lore and beliefs, were overlaid by Christianity which leavened them with the product of a more meaningful culture. The bulk of much folk lore is now an intricate admixture on to which several interpretations of Christianity have been superimposed.

Another vital element in tradition is language (see Chapter 10), which is one reason why the study of the spoken word is essential in any institution concerned with folk-life studies.

The topography of modern life is, therefore, geological in character, recent strata overlying older 'rocks' of custom and belief, some of whose outcrops still survive as gaunt primeval peaks in a much more recent social plain, some as pleasant rounded hills

[1] Sigurd Erixon: 'Regional European Ethnology', in *Folk-Liv*, I and II, Stockholm, 1937–8.

eroded by the centuries into shapes softened by the later overlying strata. In one sense, the stratum of 'sameness' laid down over the linguistic and national communities of large areas of the world during recent centuries, is a unique phenomenon. Industrial and mechanical revolutions have created dense urban growths. The invention of the internal combustion engine has brought hitherto remote communities into close contact with populous areas. Following upon this invention came the development of modern roads with the unmistakable marks of industry—and more particularly the motor industry—strewn along their uninteresting lengths like inflamed sores on a sick body. With the development of radio and television, American films and the southern English speech blare on the hearths of the most remote farmhouses in Gaelic and Welsh areas alike, in the central Welsh moorland and in the cottages of the hitherto monoglot Welsh fishermen of the Llŷn peninsula. All these innovations, in every countryside alike, have tended to destroy the social life of rural communities with a resultant considerable depopulation. At the same time swift progress in mechanical and engineering development during this century has revolutionized agricultural techniques and machinery. Consequently, the implements of the past with the technical vocabularies connected with them are rapidly disappearing in every country. In a different way, the same is true of urban life: electronics, 'modern' architecture and the like cause the materials of the life of past generations to be bulldozed away. The study of folk life, therefore, assumes the appearance of an urgent rescue operation, for a knowledge and an awareness of our past are still vital if we are to create a civilized future: *stemmata quid faciunt*.

This volume, however, is not intended as a textbook for folk-life study. It is the result of the author's personal reaction, during a working life of well over forty years in this field, to problems of folk-life study. Therefore, while there are several references, in some parts of the book, to England, Ireland and Scotland, this study is based essentially on Wales and on work dealing with Welsh folk life. I make no apology for this: not only is it the area upon which I can write with some knowledge but it must also be stressed that while much more work has to be undertaken throughout the countries of the world before Folk Life can assume the status of an academic discipline, that already achieved in many European countries (particularly in Scandinavia) as well as in America, is so vast and diverse in character that it can only be assessed by a type of polymath which the author does not claim to be.

Chapter 1

The House

'Two arts', wrote W. R. Lethaby,[1] 'have changed the surface of the world, Agriculture and Architecture . . . Architecture is the matrix of civilization.' Most professional works on the subject tend to be confined to expositions of architectural origins, to Egyptian monuments, to Babylonia, Crete and Greece, Christian and Byzantine schools, and to a consideration of Gothic throughout Europe. All this is necessary but not at the expense of excluding all discussion of the humbler homes of the ordinary people. Houses are often conditioned by their environment and in the past their materials depended on local supplies—clay, mud, pebbles, slate, stone, timber. The distribution of houses made of one or more of these materials depended to a considerable degree upon the lithology of the area.

Houses too have a way of descending the social scale. Many former mansions or manor houses have now become farmhouses or cottages (Plates 3 and 4). There is a notable example of a manor house which became a collier's cottage. It is a fact always to be remembered lest we assume that all the old farmhouses which we know today have always been farmhouses.

Early man in Britain lived in caves: in Wales, the caves of the Gower coast, for example, have provided evidence of this. In some primitive communities, screens of brushwood are known to shelter the dwellers from the weather and to protect them from wild beasts. Such was the house of the Australian aborigine. It appears reasonable to suppose that the house developed around the hearth and the family fire, whether in caves or in the open. Other—more fanciful—theories have been argued, e.g. the late Lord Raglan's

[1] W. R. Lethaby: *Architecture*, 2nd rev. ed., London, 1939, p. 7.

thesis that the house was evolved from the temple,[1] but this we reject as a general principle.

Both circular and rectangular houses existed in Britain in prehistoric times. In Wales, for instance, there is plentiful evidence of the circular type known in Britain even in Neolithic times. Traces of the type are found in several Welsh counties and proof that such houses were inhabited from at least the Early Iron Age to the Dark Ages and doubtless still later. Many of them were made of stone and fashioned after the shape of a beehive, the stonework often finished in a domical manner with a flat slab on top or a stone, which could be removed when necessary, set in the apex, the hole being sometimes used as a chimney. This type of 'beehive hut' has a wide distribution in Scotland and in Ireland where it was sometimes used until recent times for dwelling purposes. Mitchell[2] points out that some which he examined in the Outer Hebrides presented themselves 'in circumstances which do really point to a great age'. Others however were known to be quite modern: 'one, for instance, was built by a person who was alive in 1858 and there are people living' who were born in such houses. Mitchell adds that 'the meanest of all beehive houses is that which men construct at this very day, to give up-putting or shelter not to men but to pigs and poultry' in Orkney and in Caithness.

Many such pigsties have been found in south Wales (Plate 5). These are an example of a descent in the social scale, from man to pig, of a very old building technique. To quote Mitchell again, 'the beehive house certainly belongs to the man without a story, though the man with a story is found still clinging to it. It becomes thus a prolongation of the prehistoric into the historic.' In the same way, the technique of the medieval English hall continued to be used for the construction of barns.

Naturally, circular houses of early date in Wales were considerably larger than the beehive pigsty—twenty or more feet, in comparison with six feet, in diameter. And the method of roofing was often different. Many had a central post and a roof-covering of vegetable matter. Sometimes traces of a circle of posts within the

[1] Lord Raglan: *The Temple and the House.*

[2] A. Mitchell: *The Past in the Present*, Edinburgh, 1880, pp. 62–3.

house have been discovered and more than one explanation of this construction can be suggested. The archaeologists tell us that there are at least three types of such circular houses, namely, (*a*) the simple round type; (*b*) a round hut with an annexe; (*c*) a cluster of huts or 'homestead group' arranged around an open courtyard.

While the principle of communal or 'homestead' groups of houses persisted in types other than the circular houses, later evidence of round houses in Wales is scanty. Giraldus Cambrensis, in the twelfth century, writes of huts of plaited rods and of cabins of leaves made of trees with their ends plaited and of 'tents' of trees and leaves. References are found also in the literature to the 'leaf house'. The frequent references to round houses through large areas of Europe and examples of them, of plaited rods covered with leaves, grass or turf lead us to suppose that the type was well known in the Middle Ages, and indeed much later, from the Italian *capanna* to the round huts of parts of Scandinavia and of Scotland. This was the type used in Britain as elsewhere down to the present century by itinerant charcoal-burners. A writer visiting Baglan in Glamorgan on the 11th May 1800 stated: 'We here discovered a large family inhabiting a mud cabin in the form of a sugar loaf . . . These people continue here all the summer for the purpose of making charcoal.' A friend cycling through Aber-arth, Cardiganshire, about 1910, called at a house where drinks were advertised for sale to find it to be a round house with a central fire on the floor, the smoke escaping through the doorway. This was possibly the last example of the Welsh circular house of medieval and early times.

It is likely too that some of the *tai unnos* (houses built in a night) found on common land were circular though many were rectangular. In 1893 the late Sir Lleufer Thomas wrote of houses in north-west Montgomeryshire and in the neighbouring areas of Merioneth which he described as 'ink-bottle houses', that is, the chimney was central and the roof tended to be circular. They were of mud or clay with wattle partitions and straw-thatched roofs. The peat fire was in the centre of the floor and the smoke escaped through the chimney and doorway. The only house which I was able to discover conforming in any respect to Sir Lleufer's description is Abernodwydd,

Llangadfan, now in the Welsh Folk Museum (Plate 6). But it is not circular. The thatched roof approximates to an oval form with a chimney. It is in fact a rectangular timber-framed house of the hall-house type found extensively in the border counties (see below).

What, therefore, is the difference between a circular and a rectangular house? It is elementary but fundamental. In short, a rectangular house has a ridge-tree (we are not now concerned with the modern flat roof) while the circular house has not. We have indicated that the roof of the circular house can be made in several ways. If it be a stone house, the roof may be corbelled; if of stone with a straw roof, a central post may hold the apex of the roof; if it be a timber house, the timbers meet at the apex and can be bound together. There is no ridge-tree, that is, a 'tree' laid horizontally along the ridge of the roof. There is none because a circular roof has no ridge. It may thus be seen how impossible it was to extend a circular house: the only 'extension' was to build another.

* * *

The rectangular house, however, is built differently. It has two gable walls and a ridge-tree running from the one to the other. The roof is formed by laying rafters to rest on the ridge-tree and on the wall-plate of the side walls, or in a different construction (see below) on the ridge-tree and the ground. Timber-framed houses never developed beyond this stage: the principle underlying their construction has remained unchanged. But with new materials, such as reinforced concrete, the flat roof developed.

A simple and primitive method of holding the ridge-tree was to make it from pliable wood so that the two ends could be bent and placed in the earth, its major part being placed horizontally. This is a method found in some primitive communities, but apart from its typological significance it need not be considered here. The typological successor to this was to set forked posts at each end to hold the ridge-tree. When such a house had to be extended, a third forked post and a second ridge-tree could be added, so that a very long building could have a central row of forked posts and a series of ridge-trees end to end. Such houses have been known in various parts of the world. But such a construction is weak and the central posts inconvenient. In Denmark a further typological stage emerged. Pairs of sloping posts (*stridsuler*) with their ends crossing to hold the ridge-tree were placed to alternate with the central posts. This gave added strength to the structure but the numerous posts were most inconvenient. But when the alternating central posts are eliminated leaving the sloping timbers—the next typological stage—and these timbers shaped to follow the line of a vertical wall and sloping roof, the final stage was reached when the whole floor was left open for domestic use. No one suggests that all these stages of typological development were followed in any one country. While examples of all stages are known in different parts of the world, rarely do cultural elements go through the whole gamut of typological development.

Houses illustrating the last stage in this typological series, however, deserve fuller consideration. These are the houses in which the ridge-tree rests on pairs of timbers which reach from ground level to the ridge and are known as *crucks*.

The word 'cruck' is cognate with 'crutch' and there are several dialectal variants in England, Scotland and Wales. Both 'cruck' and 'crutch' have been in use, possibly because the pair of timbers uphold the roof just as a pair of crutches uphold a human body or possibly because the timbers form a *cross* to support the roof. In medieval documents, the name *sill* (*syl*[*l*]*e*) is also used for 'cruck'. In Welsh the term is *nenfforch* (lit. 'a roof fork').

In Britain, a cruck truss consists of a pair of timbers set up in inverted V form (Plate 7), the timbers generally (but not always) crossing or joining at the apex, the angle thus formed giving a fork in which the ridge-tree rests. The weight of the purlins with rafters and of the wooden wall-plates and of the whole roof-covering is therefore borne by the crucks. The walls of such a building, in contrast with other types of construction, were therefore constructionally of secondary importance and served principally only to enclose the building. They bore no constructional relationship to the roof.

In England and Wales, these crucks were always of oak. In many cases, indeed in the majority, it was at one period possible to find oak trees bent (through an outgrowing branch) in such a form that, when set up for building, part would be upright and parallel to the wall and part sloping in line with the roof. Such were possibly the great bent beams mentioned in 1278 as used for building a bake-house at Harlech Castle and in 1236 for building the kitchen at Windsor Castle.[1] In the documents these are referred to as 'great twisted beams called *crockkes*, 25 feet in length' and a phrase *furcas videlicet crockus* is also significant.

John T. Smith in an excellent study of cruck construction[2] discusses the origin and distribution of this method of building. The method, he states, 'will not fit an Anglo-Saxon or a Norman context . . . Were the origin Scandinavian, crucks would be known in those home lands if only in late derived forms, and the English distribution pattern would be different. Hence by elimination, the conformity of the cruck pattern with that of Celtic place-names may provide the answer: that both are fundamentally due to Celtic peoples. This is not necessarily to say that only Celts built crucks: it merely assigns their origin at some distant period in the British Isles to those peoples.' This, it seems to me, is a sound and satisfactory deduction. Mr. Smith illustrates further how in south-eastern England the technique 'yielded entirely to others of later continental inspiration'. It was found in those areas where the Keltic element remained strong—in Wessex, in Wales and in the north. It is also found in Scotland and in Ireland—Smith's reference to a feature in a Co. Galway church which looks 'like a transmutation of crucks into stone' is significant—and in Belgium, France, Germany, Holland and Italy.

The problem of possible Scandinavian crucks is more complex in that different writers place different emphases on the connotation of the term 'cruck'. Some of us, in considering basic typological development, rather than the craftsmanship of construction, have accepted the Danish *stridsuler* (p. 27 above) as crucks, i.e. timbers sloping from ground level to the ridge to form a fork-angle in which the ridge-tree rests, crutches to uphold the roof. This

[1] L. F. Salzman: *Building in England down to 1540*, Oxford, 1952, pp. 195 ff.

[2] J. T. Smith: 'Cruck Construction: a survey of the problems', in *Medieval Archaeology*, 8, 1964, pp. 119–51.

conforms with the exact meaning of the Welsh *nenfforch*. Smith, however, maintains that 'they are at best a collateral branch of the cruck family rather than members of it'. I have no quarrel with this conclusion provided that we are clear about the meaning of the word 'cruck' and do not confuse *species* with *genus*. My own view is that the well-developed crucks of the Welsh border country, the *stridsuler* of Denmark, the construction of the Lapp huts are all species of the genus *cruck*, but that the various species found in the British Isles are outstandingly important in their craft—and historical—context, in contrast with the more primitive Scandinavian variants.

To attempt to date the origin of cruck construction is hazardous except that one may reasonably infer that it was in early, possibly prehistoric, times. The technique persisted in a considerable number of houses in the late medieval period and to the late eighteenth century at least in some forms (e.g. the upper cruck and the 'false' hafted upper cruck, both of which did not extend to ground level). In terms of *genus*, one may say that cruck construction has been revived in the twentieth century in a modern form.

The relationship of the walls to the crucks in timber-framed houses is a matter which needs further study. Smith remarks, in discussing a house at Westick near Kamen in Germany which was occupied from the late third century A.D. until the beginning of the fifth century, that in the ground plan of the hall there are in effect two rows of post-holes close together along each of the long walls, the inner row much less numerous than the other. 'At several points two post-holes are associated, one aligned with the outer wall, the other immediately inside it. [It became evident] that . . . the inner post-hole was intended for a timber leaning inwards, the outer for a vertical post.' The excavators decided that the house was an early example of cruck construction. Smith believes that 'their conclusion is reinforced by one general point; so far as is known the cruck is the only type of roof support which, in its earlier forms, is placed immediately inside timber walls'. This is true. In passing, all such timber walls which I have seen, from the fifteenth century onwards at least, have their upright studs mortised into horizontal sills and are placed on a stone sill. Is it to be supposed that in the third century A.D., craftsmanship was so primitive that the bottom sill was left out and the upright studs merely placed in the earth?

However, Smith adds that Fox and Raglan in *Monmouthshire Houses* found that at 'the very end of cruck development . . . a wall stud stands immediately outside every cruck blade *to perpetuate this ancient structural relation*'. This is a very doubtful argument for there is no structural or constructional relation which demands

An example of modern cruck construction. *After* Friedrich Saeftel: *Krummholz- und cruck-Dachwerke in Nordwest-Europa*, pl. 77.

that a wall-stud should mask each cruck. In a late fifteenth-century Denbighshire house now in the Welsh Folk Museum, the cruck tie-beam extends beyond the cruck blade and holds the wall-plate which is notched into it (Plate 8), the tie projecting beyond the line of the timber-framed wall through the wattle-and-daub panel. In no case does the cruck stand immediately inside a wall-stud. One cannot be dogmatic except to say that in cruck-built houses, the walls were no more than 'protective screens' (to quote Fox and Raglan) fixed in more than one way to the cruck trusses and bearing no constructional relationship to the roof.

One of the richest sources of information concerning many aspects of folk life in early times are the Welsh Laws which were codified in the tenth century by Hywel Dda, 'king of all the Welsh'. Here are references to three grades of hall houses, those of the king, the freeman and the non-freeman. Various scholars have interpreted this material, with considerable unanimity. Frederick Seebohm writes of 'six well-grown trees with suitable branches apparently reaching over to meet one another . . . in two parallel rows . . . At the top each pair makes a fork upon which the roof-tree is fixed . . . At some distance back from these rows of *columns* or *forks*, low walls of stakes and wattle shut in the aisles of the house' (Plate 9).[1] T. P. Ellis describes it as 'of three parallel rows of wooden pillars, two in each row'. Sir John Lloyd writes of the king's hall as 'an oblong structure resting on six wooden uprights'. It would seem that the king's hall was built around three cruck-trusses.

This 'basilical' type of building with a nave and aisles was, as R. G. Collingwood[2] stressed, 'an early type in the Celtic world' and he and John Ward noted a number in Britain. One at Stroud near Petersfield in Hampshire had its main block divided by two rows of wooden columns. The late Sir Ian Richmond[3] noted that 'such buildings were . . . part of the Celtic heritage'. They ranged from Ireland well into Europe, and 'represent the highest level to which Celtic housing . . . attained'.

* * *

Evidence has been found in most European countries—as indeed in other parts of the world—of primitive houses which man shared with his domestic animals. Mitchell,[4] for instance, in his description of the 'black houses' of the islands of Harris and Lewis, shows how one small dwelling housed not only the family and the cattle, but included a barn to hold the fodder. This method of providing shelter for man and his beasts under the same roof had much to commend it to our early ancestors and evidence of this joint

[1] Iorwerth C. Peate: *The Welsh House*, Liverpool, 3rd ed., 1946, pp. 116 ff.
[2] ibid. [3] ibid. [4] op. cit., pp. 50 ff.

occupancy can be traced back to prehistoric times—material evidence as well as folk beliefs which must represent a long tradition. It is still held in parts of Ireland, in Scotland and in Wales that 'warmth increases the yield of milk' and that 'the cow must see the fire'. The cattle, the dogs and the poultry were indeed part of the house community, and while in some instances cattle-fodder was also stored there, it was normal in many of these 'communal' houses in Britain to store wool, cheese, apples, potatoes and corn also under the same roof.

In England and Wales, this type of house was often less primitive than the black houses of the Hebrides or the simple dwellings of the Irish countryside, although there was much similarity in lay-out and function. Many of the Welsh examples were stone cruck-built houses, and generally they were low structures from sixty to ninety feet long. Several of them in Wales are named *Tŷ Hir* (long house) and for that reason I suggested the term 'long-house' for the type. This long, low, rectangular structure has the dwelling at one end—generally the upper—and the byre at the other, the lower, end (Plates 10–11). Between the two is the principal doorway opening into the feeding-walk which is a passage-way across the centre or near centre of the house, often but not always with a doorway at its other end also. On its one side are the mangers from which the cattle feed: on the other is the entrance to the kitchen. Almost without exception the dwelling-end floor is paved up to and including the feeding-walk. The byre-end is lower and has an earthen floor.

The living-room abuts the feeding-walk from which it is entered, with a party wall between this walk and the main hearth. The party-wall, obviously a post-medieval development of a wattled frame, divides the dwelling-part from the byre but, since it does not extend across the whole breadth of the house, allows easy internal access from one end to the other. Beyond the living-room are the chamber and dairy. The creation of a loft by ceiling the ground-floor rooms at wall-plate level made possible storage of wool, cheese, corn, potatoes, apples etc., and the provision of sleeping room for the children and maid-servant(s), the men-servants usually sleeping in the stable-loft.

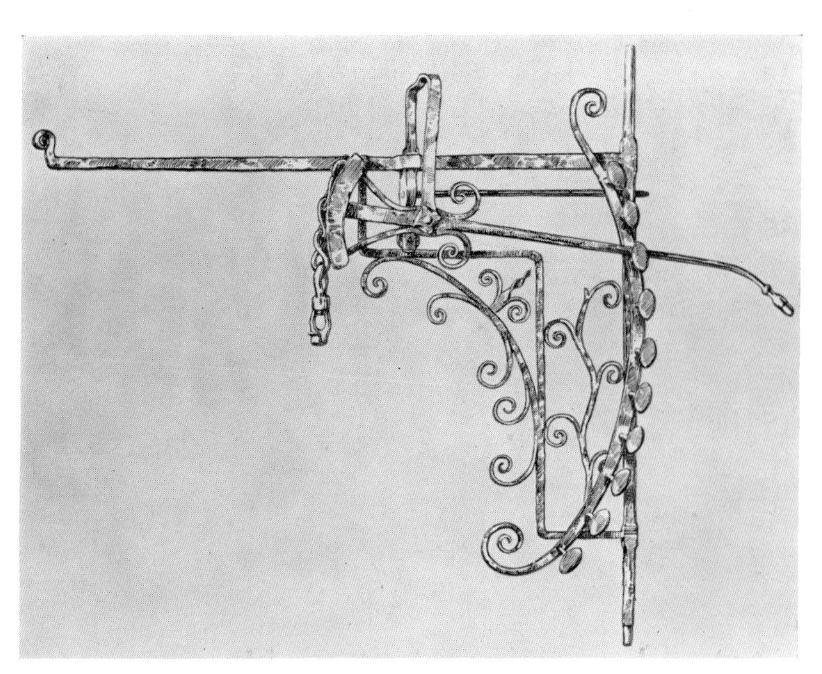

1. Lever operated pot-crane (*after* J. S. Lindsay: *Iron and Brass Implements of the English House*)

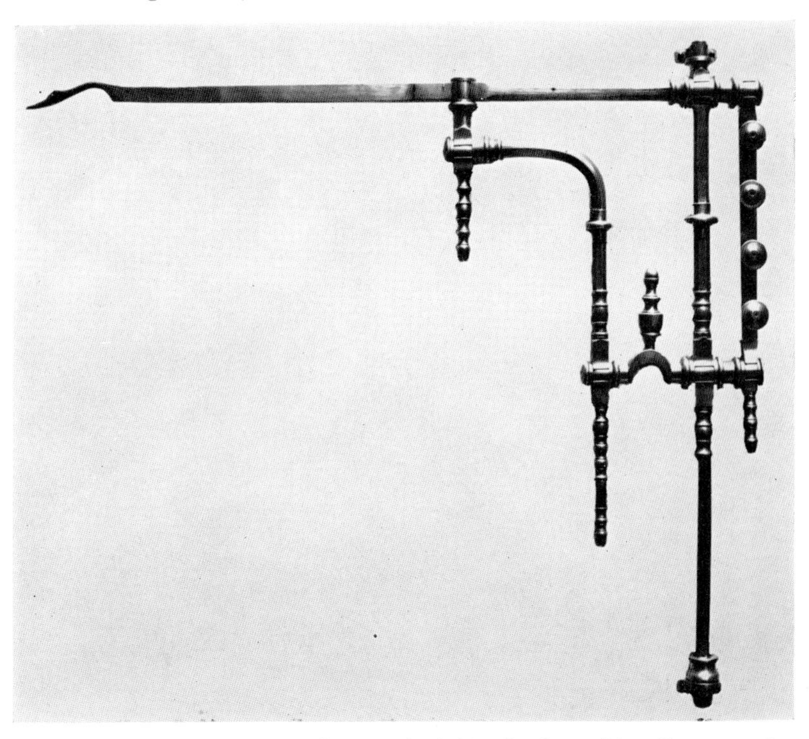

2. Pot-crane made in Llangollen, Denbighshire (in the Welsh Folk Museum)

3. Treworgan, near Raglan, Monmouthshire, in the late 18th century. From a painting in the Welsh Folk Museum

4. Treworgan today

5. Circular pigsty, Hendre, Pontypridd, Glamorgan

6. Abernodwydd, Llangadfan, Montgomeryshire (in the Welsh Folk Museum)

7. Cruck trusses

8. Crucks and timber framing, Hendre'r-ywydd Uchaf, Llangynhafal, Denbighshire (in the Welsh Folk Museum)

9. The medieval Welsh house (*after* M. Salmon: *A Source-book of Welsh History*)

There were several slight variations in the lay-out of the long-house but the essential plan was as described.

One description remains, committed to writing in the early fourteenth century but almost certainly considerably older than the manuscript in which it is found.[1] It is of 'an old hall, very black and lofty, . . . the floor uneven and full of puddles and where it sloped it was difficult to stand thereon so slippery was it with the mire of cattle. And where the puddles were, a man might go up to his ankles in water and the urine of cattle. And there were boughs of holly spread over the floor, whereof the cattle had browsed the sprigs.' The sleeping arrangements are thus described: 'And when they looked at the raised platform there was on it only a little short straw full of dust and fleas with the stems of boughs frequent in it for the cattle had eaten all the straw from head to foot.' A later reference, dated 1607,[2] from west Montgomeryshire, describes a housewife seeking 'a light to go to the lower end of the house to look to certain kine of hers'.

The long-house, now described by some writers as the byre-house, was found in most Welsh counties, in England (more especially in the north), in Scotland and in Ireland. In some cases, a straight joint appears between byre and dwelling-house and one or two recent writers have argued that this is evidence that the joint occupancy of man and his cattle is an innovation of recent date! What it does show is that houses are altered in the course of their history[3] or parts of them re-built. As Sir Cyril Fox[4] has stressed, 'spacial relationships . . . are not superficial or recent but ancient and fundamental'. No one in recent times would cut a passage-way through a gable-wall three feet thick in order to build against it a byre into which they required access. On the contrary, there are examples of such passage-ways being blocked up in order to separate the cattle from the dwelling house. The tradition of the 'communal' long-house persisted for many centuries from pre-historic times and (as Mitchell has stated in dealing with the cir-

[1] 'Breuddwyd Rhonabwy', in *Y Mabinogion.*
[2] P.R.O. MS (Wales) 4/141/3.
[3] See for example *Gwerin*, II, 1964, p. 77.
[4] In *Antiquity*, 1937, p. 438.

cular house) some were built in comparatively recent times although they were completely traditional in character. Construction of parts may sometimes be recent but such lay-outs represent a very long tradition.

* * *

The dwelling which Chaucer described in The Nun's Priest's Tale as 'ful sooty was hir bour and eek hir halle', was in the words of Hamilton Thompson,[1] 'the traditional English house, familiar in examples great and small, with its two rooms. The larger room was the hall, the smaller the bower or chamber, the first the main room of the building entered directly from outside, the second an inner and private room to which access was obtained from the hall.' This lay-out—the hall and bower—was the essential basis of the traditional English house which later developed service rooms, a screens passage and other features which varied according to the purpose and dignity of the house concerned. 'One thing and one alone,' wrote M. W. Barley,[2] 'has survived in quantity—the rural house. Here is an essential part of [the] older culture [finally killed by the Industrial and Agrarian Revolutions].' Here Barley had in mind a peasant 'society and the culture it evolved'. The Great Rebuilding which began in the second half of the sixteenth century and continued vigorously through the seventeenth into the eighteenth century altered much of the character of the English scene, while twentieth-century developments have transformed it in many areas.

The Keltic countries, however, maintained a house form even earlier typologically than the hall-and-bower; examples of it still survive in considerable numbers. This is the single-roomed rectangular cottage without the privacy of a bower, generally with a centrally placed door and a gable chimney (Plate 12). The hearth end was used as the living 'room' and the other end for sleeping.

Probably at a comparatively early stage in the history of the single-roomed house, its occupants grew aware of the need for privacy and divided the cottage interior into two by the use of

[1] A. Hamilton Thompson: *The English House*, London, 1936, p. 3.

[2] M. W. Barley: *The English Farmhouse and Cottage*, London, 1961, p. xxi.

furniture: a dresser or a clothes cupboard placed across the room could effectively conceal the sleeping space behind them, particularly if the sleeping end contained one or two cupboard beds. Such cottages remained in use in parts of Wales, as in Ireland and Scotland, down to very recent times and the writer has visited several of them. A description of cottages in Anglesey and Caernarvon in 1867 mentions cottages of 'one room about 18 or 20 feet long by 14 to 15 broad. This room is unceiled and paved with stones and is used as a living and sleeping room. It is generally partially divided by two box beds (i.e. four-post beds boarded on three sides) which are placed nearly across the centre of the room, leaving only a narrow passage to connect the portions of the room which are used by day and night respectively. Although only one room, the cottages with the beds thus disposed have the appearance of having two rooms, the backs of the beds being fitted with shelves, on which the household crockery etc. is placed.'[1] Such descriptions are numerous as were existing examples in the 1930s and later.[2]

Division by furniture was not the only method of converting the single-roomed cottage into a hall and bower. Screens of cloth, 'wisps of straw', wattle etc. were used, one screen in a Pembrokeshire cottage in 1893 being about five feet high. The obvious development from these primitive attempts at creating a two-roomed cottage was to erect partitions of laths and reeds or wattled hazel daubed with plaster. This finally resulted in a party wall with a door connecting the living and sleeping ends of the cottage. It should be noted too that even in some of the most primitive of these structures a corner of the sleeping end was sometimes partly partitioned to serve as a small dairy. A house in Radnorshire which I visited in 1936 (when it had become uninhabited) was built of dry-stone walling with a rush thatch and a ridge of grass-grown clods (Plate 13). The single room was divided by low boards into a living-room, bedroom and a small dairy. The open-hearth fireplace

[1] *Report of the Commission on the Employment of Children* . . ., 1867, p. 34.

[2] The investigators of the Royal Commission on Ancient Monuments in Wales did not seem to be aware of this when they prepared their Caernarvonshire volumes.

had a wattle-and-daub canopy above. While constructional technique is largely conditioned by environment, Sir Cyril Fox is right in his contention that 'this is not the case with lay-out' and similar lay-outs have been noticed in other parts of Wales. These single-roomed cottages represent some of 'the many strands of culture which in the Dark Ages or earlier went to the making of the social and economic pattern of rural Wales'.[1]

Another feature, found in some of the Caernarvonshire examples which illustrates a 'strand of culture' reaching back into prehistoric times, is the raised platform of slate slabs on which was placed without exception the long-case clock and the food cupboard and other valuables of the family tradition. This feature survived into larger houses, often with four bedrooms and a tiled kitchen, built late in the nineteenth century. It is, I believe, a survival of the raised platforms found in prehistoric and Dark-Age houses. While a utilitarian purpose could be argued for it in houses which had earthen floors, it was quite unnecessary on this score in tiled kitchens. But nevertheless it survived, as a feature of a distant past in the present.

The single-roomed house created problems in accommodation: the rural family unit throughout the centuries was always large and there were countless examples of overcrowding. Successive government reports refer to the 'grave evil of the want of bedroom accommodation'. One method in which this was partially overcome in such cottages was by placing boards resting across the tops of the cupboard beds in the cottage and so creating a loft over the sleeping end which could accommodate at least the small children in the family. This half-loft, almost always over the sleeping end, became widespread in Wales where it was known as a *crogloft*. It was entered by means of a ladder from the 'kitchen' floor. This extra 'room' was generally open to view from the 'kitchen' but in some instances it was boarded up, so partitioning its interior from a view of the kitchen. It is possible that the *crogloft* development is of comparatively recent date: the term itself first appeared in the Welsh language about 1760, which corroborates the argument[2] that it is a post-medieval feature.

[1] op. cit. [2] *The Welsh House*, pp. 97–8.

Modern surveys of houses in the countries of Great Britain and Ireland, such as those excellently carried out by R. Wood Jones, J. T. Smith and S. R. Jones, R. W. Brunskill and others, throw much light on developments in recent centuries of the basic house types: such developments are beyond the purpose of the present discussion, and the reader in search of such information should consult the Bibliography.

Chapter 2

The Hearth

The social centre of farmhouse and cottage life has always been the hearth and the focus of the hearth is the fire. The fire *place* of the oldest tradition in these islands was in the centre of the living-room: the family and their friends could sit around it, and not merely in front of it. The central hearth in the 'black' houses of the Hebrides and in the Highlands of Scotland and doubtless in some other areas of the Keltic countries must have helped considerably in the development of the strong oral tradition which produced there the folk tale in its full glory. 'The people's lives', writes Dr. I. F. Grant,[1] 'literally revolved round the fire', and she adds: 'It was sitting in a circle round the fire that the people listened spellbound to the telling of the old tales or took part in the good fellowship of the *Ceilidh*'. One can visualize the low benches crowded with young and old folk—low because 'the peat reek' rose in the chimneyless room leaving the air relatively clear near the ground, the company sitting below a canopy of smoke. Tall persons, as I found to my cost in a house on Lewis, could not stand in such a room for more than seconds without rushing to the doorway for a breath of fresh air. The gable hearth in this respect had its disadvantages: the company could not sit *around* the fire but in a half circle in front of it. But here again it was always in all areas of Britain and Ireland the focus of family life and the place of honour for the visiting stranger. It was the invariable custom in most areas that the fire should never be allowed to go out; this practice is still met with in the countryside. In the west Highlands of Scotland, writes Dr. Grant, 'the fire was never allowed to go out.[2] In the evening the peat fire was

[1] I. F. Grant: *Highland Folk Ways*, London, 1961, pp. 160–2.
[2] ibid.

"smoored", the ashes were drawn over the embers which in the morning were once more kindled into a glow.' In Ireland, Professor Estyn Evans writes,[1] 'the turf fire is never allowed to go out: the glowing turves are heaped with ash at night and can be readily blown into a flame in the morning.' The same is true of Wales, and in a south Cardiganshire kitchen with its very modern range and anthracite fire I have seen the master of the house manipulating 'clom balls' to cover the fire before bedtime so that 'the flame is kept in' for the morning. He explained to me triumphantly that never had his fireplace been without its fire.

This tradition of the never-to-be-extinguished fire is of great antiquity. T. P. Ellis in his monumental study[2] of the Laws of Hywel Dda, refers to the fire placed in all the houses of that time in the centre. 'At the back of the fireplace stood the fireback stone, the *pentanfaen*, and once it was placed in position it was an offence to remove it. The house itself might be destroyed, the owners might desert the site and go to another part of the country or seek other lands in the scattered acres of the tribe to cultivate, but the *pentanfaen* was never removed. It stood as a perpetual sign that the site where it stood was the site of an occupied homestead, which no one else was allowed to take possession of in such a way as to prevent the original occupiers recovering it, if they so willed. So long as the homestead was occupied the fire was never allowed to go out. Every evening the embers were raked low and a sod of peat or of earth was placed on top. In the morning the sod was removed and the embers, which had been kept glowing under the peat, were supplied with new fuel for the day's use.'

This custom persisted from the tenth century and much earlier, without any change, in Wales as in Ireland and Scotland.

Ellis refers to the fireback stone and its importance. In front of the fire, parallel with the fireback stone, was the firedog, in Welsh *pentan haearn*, the *retentaculum* of the Latin text. This held in the fire between it and the backstone (Plate 14) and across it were often fixed spits which could be turned by hand for roasting meat. The

[1] E. Estyn Evans: *Irish Heritage*, Dundalk, 1942, p. 68.

[2] T. P. Ellis: *Welsh Tribal Law and Custom in the Middle Ages*, Oxford, 1926, II, p. 164.

barred grates of a later period may well have been an echo of it.

This type of double-ended firedog is prehistoric and some early specimens found, e.g. at Capel Garmon, Denbighshire (Plate 15); Welwyn; Hay Hill between Barton and Wimpole; at Mount Bures, Essex, and at Standfordbury in Bedfordshire and also on the Continent, are all excellent examples of early Keltic art. Several of them are zoomorphic in character, the heads of each end being fashioned to represent deer or some such animals and the uprights having loops along their lengths ending in terminal scrolls above the feet. These loops were described by a fifteenth-century Welsh poet as 'rings' and the uprights as 'snakes'. The loops were used to hold the spits. He also likens the uprights to two deer.

When the central hearth gave way to the wall-hearth, the double-ended firedog gave way to pairs of three-footed single firedogs (Plate 16), these being placed one on each *side* of the fireplace: in Wales, this type had become known by the fifteenth century. Some writers have argued that the double-ended dog was used in a similar manner, particularly since more than one example appeared on some sites. But the discovery of one (as at Capel Garmon) or three (as at Welwyn) is no corroboration for their use in pairs. In the Welsh Laws, the law concerning the distribution of property between the husband and wife lays down that the husband is to have, *inter alia*, the *pentan haearn*. In every reference to this object the noun is in the singular. This iron *pentan* is important to us in order to clarify the use of the firedog. What is a *pentan*? Its present meaning is 'hob'. But 'hob' appeared in English for the first time in the early sixteenth century. Literally it means 'head of the fire' and so we have *pentanfaen*, 'the stone head-of-the-fire' and *pentan haearn*, 'the iron head-of-the-fire', the latter, furthermore, as we have seen, being rendered in Latin as *retentaculum*, 'that which holds in'. The stone 'firehead' was therefore obviously at the back, and became known as the fireback stone, the iron 'firehead' was at the front and became known as the (double-ended) firedog. The two together 'held in' the fire, the iron *pentan* alone being movable.[1]

In the course of time, with the evolution of the wall down-

[1] Iorwerth C. Peate: 'The Double-ended Firedog', in *Antiquity*, 1942, pp. 64–70.

hearth, the three-legged single firedogs used in pairs were evolved. Their uprights which appeared in the same position as those of the double-ended variety still remained vaguely zoomorphic in character and continued so throughout their use which ended in recent times.

The wall hearth made possible the suspension above the fire of a cooking utensil. This produced the pot-crane or sway (see Plates 1, 2) which could be fixed to the wall. Here again the name 'crane' led some craftsmen to indulge in zoomorphic designs.

The utensil most often suspended from the crane was an iron cooking pot with three short feet. These pots used throughout Britain and Ireland are descended from the bronze cauldrons which, as Estyn Evans has noted, ranged in date over a thousand years from about 700 B.C. to A.D. 1700. In the early Welsh Laws the cauldron, 'indispensable' like the harp, was of great value.

The baking pot is, in some respects, a more interesting utensil than the all-purpose cauldron. This too often has three short feet but unlike the cauldron it always has a lid. In English a baking pot, it is called in Welsh *ffwrn*[1] ('oven') and in Irish *bácús* (? bake-house),[2] which has the same meaning. The late Åke Campbell states that the Irish fireplace was of 'pure hearth-type no trace whatever being evident of the influence of the built-in oven culture. It stands in direct contrast with the Middle—and especially East-European tradition where the stone-built oven completely dominates the fireplace, indeed even the whole kitchen. Thus Ireland is in this respect the antithesis to Finland and Russia'. The same is true of Wales where the built-in oven, generally of earthenware, was a late importation. I have seen several examples in south Wales bearing the marks of makers south of the Bristol Channel. The baking pot (Plate 17) differs from the cooking-pot in that its sides are straight and not curved and has a lid which is flat or almost flat. In the Welsh Laws, *y badell a'r trybedd* ('pan—or pot—and tripod) were the wife's property. When, as was often the case, the pot had no feet, it was generally placed on a tripod.

[1] It has several other names differing according to locality, e.g. *callor, cetel, crochan pobi, padell.*

[2] In *Folkliv*, 1937, pp. 207–34.

The methods of using the baking pot varied in detail,[1] but generally, in bread-making, the dough was placed in the pot, the lid put on and the pot placed in the glowing peat, which was also placed around the pot and over the lid. Informants in Cardiganshire and Montgomeryshire, for example, told me that about 1900 they baked loaves, sponges, cakes and tarts in this way and roasted 'spare-rib on potatoes'. It was 'far better than any from the modern bakeries'. A farmer on the Pumlumon moorland mentioned that they had no other oven of any description in the house.

Where peat was scarce or unobtainable, dried cowdung, gorse twigs and fern were used. Where the down-hearth fire had given way to a grate, the baking was often done with fern *on the hob*. In some instances the dough was placed on a griddle-iron, a flat circular iron plate placed on a tripod, and the pot inverted over it.

Cooking was often done outside the house. A hole was made in the ground, considerably larger than the baking pot. It was well lined with glowing peat from the house fire, the pot put in with its lid on and then completely covered with burning peat. Mr. Ffransis G. Payne informs me that in one locality in south Cardiganshire baking had been done outside a cottage on an outcrop of bare rock. The rock was brushed clean and the pot inverted over the loaves. The fuel was chiefly furze and it was believed that if the fire were kindled with straw from the same threshing as the grain from which the flour was ground, the bread would be sweeter.

This practice of outdoor baking and roasting may explain why in each case where a house has been removed for re-erection in the Welsh Folk Museum no kind of indoor oven was discovered except in a house from Radnorshire. Indeed in the case of one house we were told that the 'oven' was 'in the field outside' but no details of it could be discovered. The former existence of a separate outside 'place' for baking may account for the general use of the term *popty* (lit. bakehouse) for 'oven' in parts of north Wales.

The hooks used for suspending utensils above the fire, of which there are many variants, can all be paralleled by examples dating from the Early Iron Age and Romano-British times and betoken the same continuity of tradition characteristic of so many elements in

[1] Iorwerth C. Peate: 'The Pot-oven in Wales', in *Man*, 1943, no. 3.

our culture. Roasting on spits or wooden skewers had the same long history: these were turned by hand in front of the open fire. The iron spit developed a handle on one end and was probably the type attached to the double-ended firedog. Later a flanged wheel on the spit was evolved to hold a chain which was attached to a large wooden wheel-drum mounted above the fireplace. In this was placed a low long-bodied dog, of the 'turnspit breed' (Plate 18) which, remaining inside the wheel-drum at its bottom, pawed it around so turning the spit attached by the chain to it. This development originated in classical times and persisted in Wales into the nineteenth century. Dr. Caius, founder of Caius College, Cambridge, writing about the middle of the seventeenth century, stated that the dogs 'go into the wheel, which they turning about with the weight of their bodies, so diligently look to their business that no drudge nor scullion can do the feat more cunningly, whom the popular sort hereupon term turnspits.'[1]

Later developments, in the seventeenth and eighteenth centuries, were the weight-driven spit-jack and the wrongly called smoke jack which had 'paddles' in the chimney which were driven by the upward rush of hot air and could work dangle spits as well as the horizontal spits. These existed until spits ceased to be used. Simple dangle spits suspended on a cord which twisted and untwisted slowly were often assisted by two weighted 'fliers'. The type was eventually superseded by the clockwork jack deriving its power from a spring wound up like that of a watch or clock. All these mechanical devices were far removed from the simple hand-rotated spit of the double-ended firedog.

It would be tedious to enumerate the many implements used on the hearth and in the kitchen: this has been admirably done by Seymour Lindsay (op. cit. supra) and by other writers. Reference should be made however to some which illustrate well the persistence of tradition in all folk communities. Prehistoric remains discovered in many excavations have thrown light on early methods of cooking and of the preparation of food. During pre-Roman times in Britain, crops of wheat, barley and beans were raised; oxen,

[1] Quoted by J. Seymour Lindsay: *Iron and Brass Implements of the English house*, London, 1927, p. 52.

sheep, pigs, dogs, horses and hens were brought into the service of man. Deer, wolves, swans, cranes and wild duck were hunted. Spinning and weaving were practised: sloes and blackberries picked, flour ground and bread baked. Spoons, ladles, wooden bowls and iron knives were used. In brief, the foundations of the life and culture which flourished later were then laid. The Romans introduced such birds as the guinea fowl, the turtle dove and the peacock, fruit such as mulberry and quince, walnut and filbert as well as vegetables and herbs. Amongst the cooking implements of the period was the flesh-hook, a triple barbed hook (Plate 19) for raising pieces of meat from a cauldron. Medieval examples of these hooks are known and examples survived in Wales to the nineteenth century.

In the Dark Ages, as the late Sir Ifor Williams has pointed out,[1] soldiers at a 'feast' sat around a *trull*, a vessel holding liquor. They drank from a *pann* (which is Keltic and not an English borrowal). Wine was drunk from vessels of glass, gold or silver; mead and ale from horns. All these details are mentioned in the Aneirin poems of the sixth century which refer to the 'North' extending from York to Edinburgh and Strathclyde. The men of these poems sowed corn, ploughed, fished, hunted deer, wild pig and grouse. They herded cattle and lit their halls with rushlights and pine torches. They had kitchen gardens and showed a fondness for apples. Trivets (*try-beddawd*) are mentioned as well as baths, the latter inherited probably from Roman culture. The development of the Christian church had considerable effect upon cooking: for example, the introduction of fast days increased the use of fish and the development of fish-ponds, while the discovery of the 'unique value' (as Ainsworth-Davis puts it) of Trent water by the monks for brewing purposes led to the foundation of Burton Abbey in 1002.

A knife was part of the equipment of every man and was doubtless used at meals for a long time for it was only in the seventeenth century that a knife and fork were placed on the table in front of each person. Thomas Coryat of Odcombe travelling in Italy in 1611 noted with surprise the fashion of placing a fork before each man. 'Hereupon I myselfe thought good to imitate the Italian

[1] Sir Ifor Williams: *Canu Aneirin*, Cardiff, 1938, pp. lx–lxiii.

fashion by this forked cutting of meate, not only while I was in Italy, but . . . oftentimes in England since I came home.' The earliest known silver fork used for this purpose in Britain bears the hall-mark 1632 and its coming marked the end of the pointed table-knife.[1]

To return to the prehistoric period, the lake dwellings of central Europe from Neolithic times down to the Early Iron Age have yielded evidence of wooden tubs, plates, spoons and ladles. Glastonbury, occupied in the Early Iron Age, yielded 'a miscellaneous collection of wooden objects of a most interesting description, which not only throws considerable light upon the skill and capabilities of the inhabitants but also upon the art and state of culture of pre-Roman Britain'.[2] These included tubs and ladles. The ladles have hooked handles and bear a close resemblance to those of the Swiss lake dwellings on the one hand and to the products of the present-day Welsh turners on the other. Here is a piece of kitchen equipment which has persisted unchanged for almost three thousand years—unchanged because it combines artistry of design with fitness for purpose.

[1] C. T. P. Bailey, *Knives and Forks*, London, 1927, p. 7.

[2] A. Bulleid and H. St. George Gray: *The Glastonbury Lake Village*, 1911, p. 310.

Chapter 3

The Home

We have already seen how the house, in each of its many forms, consisted of a living room and one or more bedrooms, and that a dairy was also an essential part of a farmhouse. Let us now consider how these houses were furnished and equipped to make them into homes.

FURNITURE

The type and quality of furniture throughout the centuries depended greatly on the raw materials available. We read how in Ireland 'good craftsmanship in wood is so rarely seen in the Irish peasant house that one easily notices a piece of quality furniture. The chances are that it has come out of the "big house" or near the coast, from a wrecked ship . . . The truth seems to be that by the time improved styles of furniture and settled conditions of life had come about in the second half of the seventeenth century, the native oakwoods had been almost everywhere destroyed and the common furniture came to be made of bog wood or imported soft wood.'[1] To some extent in some districts of Scotland the same poverty of furniture was found. But in Wales as in England the picture was very different. In these countries there was an abundant supply through the centuries of oak, ash, beech and birch, and indeed of pine, larch and such softwoods.

Furniture of the medieval period was scarce and remains chiefly in churches. The absence of references to furniture in the Welsh Laws is notable: the word *cist* ('chest') stands alone amongst references to tubs, vats, churns and such equipment. The chest was

[1] E. Estyn Evans, *Irish Folk Ways*, London, 1957, p. 85.

a basic element of early furniture: it could hold meal, flour, bed linen, clothes etc. It could also be used as a seat. Undoubtedly the earliest form was the dug-out type (Plate 20), made from a single tree trunk and hollowed out. The example illustrated came from a Montgomeryshire church where for many centuries it had been used to keep the church plate and documents. It may well date to about A.D. 1200. Such simple forms of this period were universal and can be found in every country in Europe. It was a period of a basic uniformity of design. With the development of house furniture national and regional individuality of design began to develop, but with the ravages of the beetle, the instability of persons and the vagaries of time, wooden objects of any great age had a habit of disappearing. The churches, however, with their continuity of tradition, preserved their medieval furniture to a much greater extent.

From the solid hollowed-out chest a variety of dissimilar objects evolved, such as the settle, the chest of drawers and one form of chair. The development of the solid chest itself resulted in the framed chest, generally with an ark-shaped lid which itself when upturned and carried on two poles was used as a handbarrow to carry sacks of meal etc., into the chest. This type (Plate 21) was found in the thirteenth century and continued to be produced with little development or variation into the nineteenth century if not, occasionally, later. It also had a wide distribution. Well known in Britain, it is also to be found as far afield as Rumania and Bulgaria where I found it being used in much the same way as in Wales.

In later years the front and ends of the chest were used for decoration, mostly carved. With this development the close dating of such pieces of furniture became possible, though instances are known where dated pieces show that in some areas types of construction and decoration persisted long after they had disappeared in the fashionable circles. For example, a chest of drawers from Glamorgan which is dated 1717 has all the features of the fashions of 1670 and would undoubtedly be so dated if the piece itself did not bear a date nearly fifty years later. Another chest from Monmouthshire is inscribed *Sarah Ward Her Chest 1722* (Plate 22) but is obviously considerably earlier, the explanation being that the central panel bearing the inscription can be seen (from the inside) to have been inserted in 1722 and ornamented in the style of the older panel for which it was substituted. Another example known to me is an oak panel carved with Renaissance ornament, and foliage in the spandrels embodying Gothic tradition, which on style would be dated about 1525. But in the centre is a carved representation of a seal which is dated 1590 and the complete specimen must be post-1590 in date.

The persistence of older fashions of decoration in some areas is admirably illustrated in the case of 'black and white' chequer inlay in holly and bog oak, a type of decoration which disappeared in fashionable circles during the last quarter of the seventeenth century. But in several parts of Wales it remained popular throughout the eighteenth century and well into the nineteenth century.

The presence of such examples have before now led to dangerous generalizations about dating. It has been widely held that in 'remote' areas such as Wales and the Highlands of Scotland—remote, that is, from the metropolitan centre, London—there was a time-lag in fashion and that therefore the poor benighted Welsh and Scots were, until recent times, a century behind in their fashions. Nothing could be further from the truth. In medieval times, for instance, both those countries had close contacts with France and the European world. The fifteenth-century literature of Wales tells of tables loaded with the choicest of foreign fruits and with the wines of Rochelle, Bordeaux and Gascony. The tapestries of Arras are described and 'gold adorned chairs', crystal windows and many other details of much sophistication mentioned. Generalizations about dating can be extremely dangerous.

When a drawer or a pair of drawers were added as a lower stage of the chest it acquired a hybrid quality and became known as a 'mule chest'. With this development the way was now free to the evolution of the chest-of-drawers and later the tallboy (sometimes called a 'chest-upon-chest').

As John Gloag has stressed,[1] the origin and meaning of the word 'cupboard' is a difficult problem but contemporary records 'indicate that the word meant exactly what it sounded like—a board for cups'. One must not be misled by the term 'board'. In Welsh *bwrdd*

[1] John Gloag: *A Short Dictionary of Furniture*, London, 1952, p. 17.

10. Cilewent, Dyffryn Claerwen, Radnorshire (in the Welsh Folk Museum): exterior

11. Cilewent: interior showing view of cowhouse from the kitchen

12. A one-roomed cottage, Llainfadyn, Rhosgadfan, Caernarvonshire (in the Welsh Folk Museum)

13. A primitive one-roomed cottage, Radnorshire

14. Central hearth, Hendre'r-ywydd Uchaf, Denbighshire (in the Welsh Folk Museum). *Photo: Dafydd Peate*

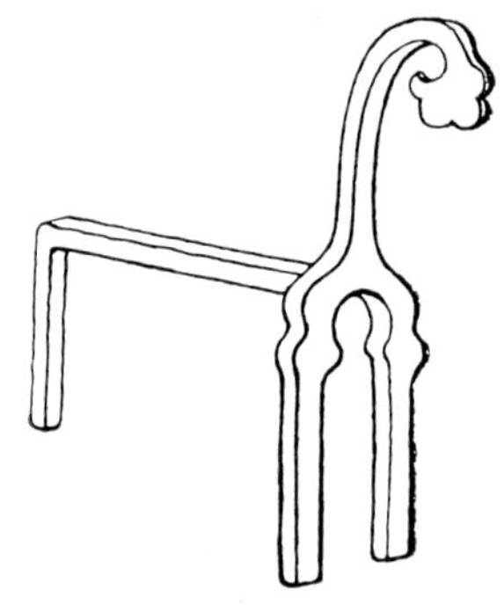

16. Single firedog

15. Firedog, Early Iron Age, Capel Garmon, Denbighshire (in the National Museum of Wales, Cardiff). *Photo: National Museum of Wales*

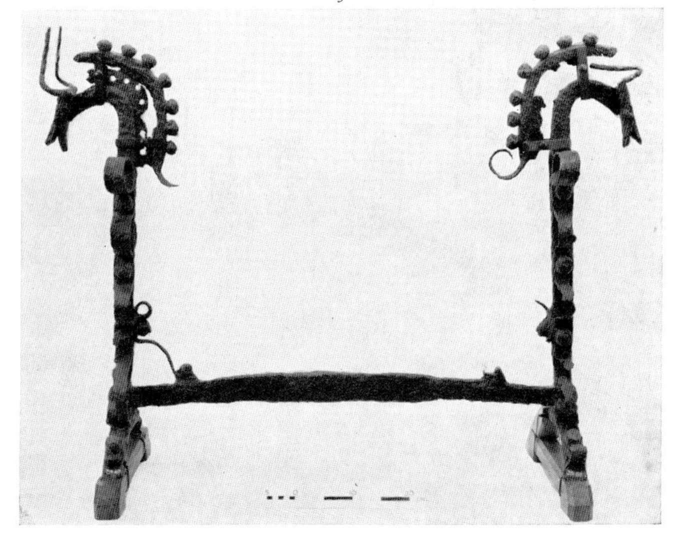

17. Baking pot (in the Welsh Folk Museum)

18. Turnspit dog in action, west Wales (*after a Rowlandson drawing*)

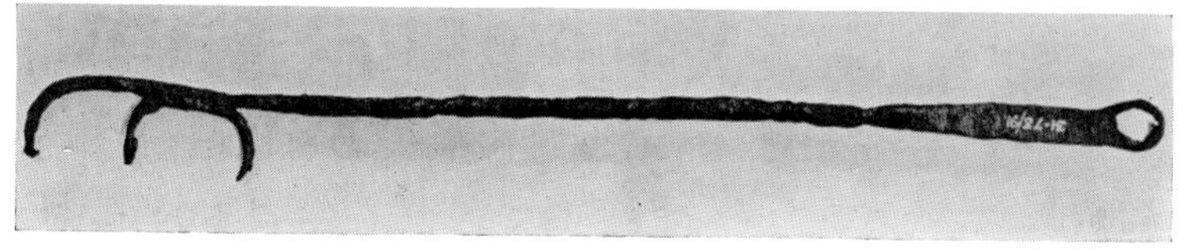

19. A 'flesh-' or meat-hook from Monmouthshire (in the Welsh Folk Museum)

or *bord* ('board') is the term for 'table' and in English in medieval times board and table were synonymous terms. It has been shown by R. W. Symonds[1] and others that the original form of the cupboard was a board (table) upon which vessels containing drink could be set down and household plate displayed. In the sixteenth century when they appeared these 'boards' developed a lower shelf and these open shelves for holding cups and displaying plate were called in that century *court cupboards*. This term in the past has been incorrectly applied to the press cupboard which is a large cupboard in two stages, the lower consisting of two large compartments with a shelf above and smaller cupboards behind it. When the upper and lower stages were of separate construction and open to be dismantled when necessary the cupboard was known in Wales as a *cwpwrdd deuddarn* (lit. 'two-piece cupboard'). Its further development was to place a canopy above its upper stage, so providing extra display space. This converted the two-piece into a three-piece cupboard: in Wales this was an extremely popular piece of furniture from the sixteenth to the nineteenth century: the cupboard acquired the adjective *tridarn* ('threepiece') which has passed into the vocabulary[2] of the English language.

Movable chairs were known in Britain before the Norman conquest and throughout the Middle Ages[3] but they were scarce. At that time, chairs were symbols of authority and it appears[4] that fourteen officers of the Welsh Court may have held chairs: the chief bard certainly did. The importance attached to this practice is still commemorated by the term 'Chairman' for the person who sits at the head of a 'board'. Representations are found, in Saxon and medieval illuminated manuscripts, of throne-like structures of fantastic church-stall dimensions which must have been the seats of persons of exalted rank and were therefore few.

It has therefore been suggested that they were evolved from the chest by the addition of a panelled back and solid panelled sides which in spite of their bulk sometimes accompanied the owner in

[1] *The Connoisseur*, 1943. [2] See for instance Gloag, op. cit., p. 483.

[3] Ralph Edwards in *A History of the English Chair*, London, 1951, p. 5, refers to a *cathedra mobilis* in a royal writ of Henry III.

[4] Cott. MS Titus D iii and Peniarth MS 32.

his travels from house to house. An inventory dated 1466 states that the Duke of Suffolk travelling to Oxfordshire had a 'chair of timber of estate' with a leather case into which it could be packed when taken to pieces. It seems reasonable to suppose that some of the earliest surviving domestic chairs must have been evolved from the chest by the addition of a panelled back and sides (Plate 23). The earliest of the surviving examples belong to the first quarter of the sixteenth century.

It should be remembered however that the box chair was certainly not the only type of early chair and that not all forms of chairs owed their development to the chest. An illustration in Peniarth MS. 28 (in the National Library of Wales), which is a Latin manuscript of the Welsh Laws, shows the Judge of the Court sitting in a four-legged chair (Plate 24), the back of which scarcely reaches his shoulders. This manuscript (with its illustrations) was written about 1180. The chair illustrated in it may well have been evolved from the stool and it may not be without significance that the Welsh words for 'chair' throughout a great part of south Wales is not *cadair* but *stôl*.

Another type of early chair, with a triangular seat (like one form of stool) with three legs, was the 'turned' chair, a variety, to quote Edwards, 'of great antiquity and wide geographical distribution which remained in favour until a much later date'. The whole structure of these chairs (with the exception of course of the seat) was turned on a lathe. Various theories have been adduced concerning the origin of this type: the least likely is that it is of Scandinavian origin. Another suggestion is that it is of Byzantine origin: I have seen examples in the Balkan countries. But it may well have evolved from the all-turned stool. A development is an example (Plate 25) in the Welsh Folk Museum; it has four legs, a rectangular seat and is of almost throne-like proportions. It comes from a mansion in Carmarthenshire where it was known as 'the Justice's Chair': whether this betokens an ancient tradition is a matter for conjecture. There is a similar chair in the President's lodging at Queen's College, Cambridge.[1] It is associated with Erasmus and may well be early sixteenth century in date.

[1] M. Harris: *The English Chair*, London, 1937, p. 8.

The panel-back oak armchair with carved cresting and with stretchers which became fashionable about 1600 was extremely popular in Wales. When the practice was instituted in the nineteenth century of awarding chairs for poetry at the various Welsh *eisteddfodau*, this was the type most often seen. I have in my possession an eisteddfod chair made and awarded in 1923 which is an oak panel-back armchair complete with stretchers of a type which could be seen in the early years of the seventeenth century!

Another type of chair found in Wales and also in Scandinavia and parts of western Europe is a covered type made entirely of straw strengthened underneath with a slight wooden framing (Plate 26). The straw is coiled, as in the making of a bee-skip, and the coils are bound together with strips of bramble bark. This type of work, found in baskets, seedlips, cradles, grain measures and other miscellaneous objects for domestic use, is called *lip* and is cognate with Danish *løb*. The only tools used in making and binding the coils are a section of a cow's horn through which the straw is passed to maintain a consistent diameter of the coil, and a needle for binding made from a bone from a horse's leg. This simple country craft must be of great antiquity as its distribution suggests. The type of chair so made is known as *cadair telynor* (harpist's chair). The word appears in the English dictionaries as *leap* which is used dialectically for many types of baskets, but particularly of wicker-work.

Another element in the traditional life of the home is the bed. In early times the family slept on the floor on straw or rushes. Giraldus Cambrensis, writing in the twelfth century, in his description of Wales, writes of the family sleeping on a bed common to all, placed along the side of the house and made of rushes, finely plaited and covered with a hard rough cloth made locally. Their clothes at night, he added, were the same that they used in the daytime—a shirt and a thin mantle. But he explains too that in the common bed their feet were near the fire which, as we have already noted, was alight throughout the night. Estyn Evans's[1] account of the sleeping arrangements of the peasant population of Mayo and Donegal as late as the eighteenth century, is almost precisely similar to

[1] *Irish Folk Ways*, p. 86.

Gerald's description of twelfth-century Wales: the practice in the Highlands of Scotland appears to have been similar, even in the eighteenth century—'the humblest folk still often slept on heather with blankets'![1]

Reference has already been made to a platform accommodating the sleeping-place. This was known in Welsh as the *tyle* and the Laws refer to *gobenyd tyle* (the *tyle* bolster). This was probably the precursor of the bed raised above ground level and the term *erchwyn* (side of a bed) found in the early poetry presupposes a side over which you would *fall*.

Wooden beds were found in medieval times and references are made in a Welsh work of the thirteenth century to *gwelyeu pren* (wooden beds) and to the woodwork of 'raised' beds (*gwelyeu dyrchauat*). The history of the development of the bed in post-medieval times need not concern us here, but some features are important to the theme of this book.

The cupboard bed is of considerable antiquity and of wide distribution throughout Europe, and particularly the Atlantic fringes. Estyn Evans discusses 'the relationship between the parental bed and the fire' in the traditional house of north-west Ireland where a small outshot accommodated the bed at the chimney end.[2] These wall-beds, for they may be thus described, appeared in Ireland, the Orkneys, the Faroes, the Hebrides and western Scotland and in other countries. They may well be directly descended from the platform beds of the circular houses of prehistoric and protohistoric times. In later periods, these beds became wooden cupboard beds, with doors which could be closed in the daytime, the 'parental' bed in Wales (as in Ireland) being near the fire (Plate 27) though in the two-roomed cottages this was often not the case. Dr. Grant states that in the Highlands it was in the eighteenth century that 'box-beds' became common.[3]

With the development in Wales of the bedchamber in farmhouse and cottage, more handsome beds became known. The bedchamber on the ground floor was usually reserved for the visiting

[1] I. F. Grant: op. cit., pp. 168–9.
[2] *Irish Folk Ways*, p. 69.
[3] ibid.

guest and was lavishly furnished. A farmhouse in Radnorshire with loft bedrooms had a four-poster bed (now in the Welsh Folk Museum) (Plate 28) with the head-board carved with the owner's name and the date 1658, geometrical designs and a figure (holding a bow in one hand and an arrow in the other) entitled DEATH. This was truly a grim setting for the nightly occupant, and a surprising precursor of the framed biblical texts of Victorian times. But of course James Price, the farmer, may have been one of the early Dissenters for whom to die was but to sleep!

Much information concerning house furniture and its disposition in the various rooms can be gleaned from the many inventories preserved in manuscript collections: some of these have been printed. Most of these relate to mansions and large houses. But occasionally inventories of smaller houses appear, e.g. a Merioneth upland house in 1685 is inventoried as follows:

'All chests and wooden vessels in the cellar, £3. 4s. 0d., all the beds and chests in the room above the kitchen, £2; one cupboard, five chairs and ten mortised stools, in the parlour, £1.'[1]

In the nineteenth century, the 'dowry' of a Cardiganshire farming couple was described in a poem.[2] The poem is in Welsh and refers to the fact that all the furniture was of oak or ash. 'My mother had an oak linen-press cupboard, my father a corner cupboard and a "crooked dresser" to fit the corner. There were three meal chests, wonderfully big with large arched lids [see above, p. 47], a washing tub, a kneading trough, a milk tub, a butter-milk pan, and a wooden butter tray; a car to hold the barley bread, another to hold spoons, a wooden board to hold trenchers and bowls,' and so on in great detail.

The reference to oak and ash as the timber used for furniture is of particular interest. In isolated societies in rural England, in Scotland, Wales or in Ireland, furniture depended largely upon the material available. We have already noted (p. 46) how in Ireland,

[1] (Ralph Edwards, and Iorwerth C. Peate,): *Welsh Furniture from Tudor to Georgian Times: Catalogue*, Cardiff, 1936, p. 7.

[2] Iorwerth C. Peate: *Diwylliant Gwerin Cymru*, 3rd Ed., Liverpool, 1946, pp. 129–30.

where the native oakwoods had been almost everywhere destroyed, the common furniture came to be made of bog wood and imported soft wood and how in certain areas of Scotland the same poverty of furniture was evident. In Wales however there was an abundance of oak and ash: good solid pieces continued to be made throughout the centuries without any dependence on the luxury of imported woods. Furniture made from mahogany or walnut down to the end of the eighteenth century—and indeed later—was generally to be found only in the mansions. An upland farmer's furniture would often be made from timber grown on his farm. I have seen in a mid-Wales farmhouse a magnificent sideboard and a long-case clock made in the eighteenth century from locally grown oak cleverly stained through the use of 'bull's blood' to resemble mahogany.

Continuity of tradition, a characteristic feature of so many strands of folk life, is well-illustrated in the story of Welsh country furniture. The press cupboard (both the two-piece and three-piece varieties) which were so fashionable in the seventeenth century continued to be made into the nineteenth century, with due regard of course to changing styles and proportions: a late eighteenth-century example is illustrated (Plate 29). Inlaid decoration, fashionable in Elizabethan times, continued in use in Wales well into the nineteenth century. Continuity of tradition was to be seen too in another form. It may be illustrated by the following example. The will, proved in 1776, of a Merioneth upland farmer mentions

> 'Item, my daughter Alice David: an oak chest that lies in the room above the stable.'

In 1914 the chest was still 'in the room above the stable' when it was acquired for the collection of a member of the same family.

THE DAIRY

Dairying had its own special equipment—sycamore bowls, wooden jugs (known by a variety of dialectal terms in English as in Welsh and other languages), ewers, sieves, butter workers etc. Reference has already been made (Chapter 2) to the hooked spoons and ladles of prehistoric ancestry, all of which were necessary elements in the equipment of the dairy. Another utensil used both in the dairy and on the table was the wooden piggin made of staves bound together, one stave being longer and shaped at the top to form a handle. In many instances, these piggins used for holding and drinking milk, butter-milk and other liquids were generally bound with metal bands. But a popular type was the stave piggin bound with a broad band (of the height of the piggin itself) of thin wood, the ends of which were so shaped as to interlock (Plate 30) and hold the complete structure of the vessel securely and tightly in position. This method of piggin-binding is found in various European countries. Welsh emigrants (and doubtless others) took the technique to America where it was found in the eighteenth and nineteenth centuries.[1]

Churns (Plates 31–33) were generally of four types, the swinging churn, the knocker or plunger churn, the box churn, and the rotary barrel type which became common during the last century. The most primitive form of swinging churn resembled a wooden pail, two of the staves extended with holes in their terminals to allow a grip for swinging the churn. A 'stave churn' (*buddei ystyllawt*) is mentioned in the Welsh Laws. The churning was done by swinging the 'pail' to and fro in front of the body. It must have been a laborious process. A more practical swing or rocker churn was a rectangular box with slats fixed across inside. This was mounted on a stand and having a central fitting only could be swung or rocked on its axis, its contents being churned to and fro between the slats. The knocker or plunger churn, again made of oak staves, was much the same shape as the modern metal milk-churns. Conical, and of lengths varying from one to three feet, it was often beautifully shaped, the staves being hooped with metal bands. The removable lid had a hole in its centre through which a knocker pole was inserted, having at its base a circular or cruciform holed wooden pad. The churning was effected by the up-and-down movement by hand of this knocker. The type was widely distributed throughout Europe, and in many areas had hoops of split hazel or rowan instead of the later iron. The box churn was a rectangular box about two

[1] Iorwerth C. Peate: 'Welsh Piggins', in *The Connoisseur*, 1930, pp. 310–11.

and a half feet long, two feet wide and two feet deep. An iron handle attached at the side to an axle bar which passed through the churn turned a four winged 'fan' inside. Each of these wings was made of horizontal slats fitted in frames; by turning the handle the milk was churned through the wings. The rotatory churn (which is chronologically much later than the other types) was barrel shaped and on a stand. The whole churn was rotated.

In many countries power for working some of these types of churns was developed. Water power was often used, in others the dog or horse. Examples of churns worked by dogs survived in Wales until about 1940 (Plate 33). A box churn was attached by a long iron spindle to a circular wooden table lying at an angle of about forty-five degrees. Strips of wooden beading were fixed at regular intervals on the surface of the circular table on which the dog or dogs were placed. The animals on leashes pawed the table around, the beading giving each paw a firm hold. The dog remained more or less stationary but continued to paw, keeping the table turning under its feet. It was geared to the churn in such a way that the four-winged fan inside rotated quickly and the churning was soon completed. The dogs were well-cared for and in the only dog-churning which I witnessed, they could only be kept away from the churn-table with difficulty so anxious were they to continue the exercise.

Butter prints and boxes afforded the wood carver an opportunity of practising his craft and the pound and half-pound prints bore designs of many kinds—representations of cows and of birds being especially popular. To prepare these small units, the butter had to be well 'worked' to rid it of all butter-milk still remaining in it. For this purpose, butter-working tables were made. These resembled in shape the shields on the Bayeux tapestry, having a pointed base and a rounded top. Around the perimeter of this table a groove was cut ending at the base of the table-top which was set on three legs. The butter-maker worked the butter on the table, the milk running into the groove and along it to a pail below.

Cheese-making was also part of the work carried on in the dairy. Most cheese-presses consisted of a low bench on to which was mortised a frame for holding a heavy weight which could be lowered by a screw device on to the wooden 'vat' (on the bench) holding the cheese, the purpose here again being to extract all moisture from the cheese. In the more primitive forms, the weight consisted of a heavy block of stone with a flat base to fit on to the top of the vat. The windlass type of press with a wooden box in which a number of stones could be placed according to the weight required was a development to be found in the eighteenth century. These windlass-box presses were often made of oak and the box panelled (Plate 34). By the latter half of the following century, cast-iron cheese presses began to supplant the traditional types.

LIGHTING

Technological developments in the twentieth century have been so phenomenal that it is difficult for the younger generation today to imagine how primitive was the lighting of the farmhouse and cottage even fifty years ago. And yet apart from an interlude of a century (from the 1820s to the 1920s) when a chemical method of fire-lighting was in vogue, the traditional method of kindling a fire has persisted from early prehistoric times to this day. We do not know when methods of fire-kindling were first evolved in prehistoric times, but undoubtedly the discovery must have revolutionized man's life. Here at last was a weapon to keep marauding wild animals at bay, a means of changing man's diet through the development of cooking and of modifying even his facial structure by providing him with cooked meals instead of the tough raw meat and vegetables that he had previously to tear with his teeth.

The traditional method of obtaining fire in most parts of western Europe was by percussion, a method illustrated by the sparks kindled when the hoof of an iron-shod horse strikes a stone. For this purpose in early prehistoric times in Europe the agents employed were iron pyrites and flint or quartz: they were used too by the Eskimo and some north American Indians. In the course of time, the metal iron superseded its ore. This led to the development of the flint and steel method of striking a light. From the Early Iron Age down to 1826 the flint and steel remained the common method of striking a light in Britain. In 1826 however the friction match was introduced by John Walker of Stockton-on-Tees: it consisted of small strips of wood or pasteboard, tipped with various chemicals which made it, when drawn through a piece of folded sandpaper, produce a light. Various types of friction matches had become popular by 1834 and in 1855 came the safety match invented by a Swede named Lindstrom. The match has remained in use for over a century. But early in the twentieth century a return was made to the traditional flint and steel method in the shape of the petrol lighter and the gas lighter, these being merely improvements on the old flint, steel, and tinder. The modern gas lighter is the direct descendent of the iron pyrites and flint of the Early Iron Age.

The traditional 'steel' was roughly U-shaped and held around the fingers of one hand much like a 'knuckle-duster'. A piece of flint was held in the other hand and when struck sharply together the steel and flint produced sparks. To catch these sparks, tinder made of charred rags was used. From the smouldering tinder blown upon after a wood splinter or some such material was placed in it a flame was obtained.

The three elements of the 'strike-a-light'—flint, steel and tinder—were generally kept in a tinder box with compartments for each. Many forms of tinder boxes were made. Most kitchens had fairly large wooden tinder boxes or metal candlesticks with a box under the base of the sconce. A very common form was a round tin box with a candle sconce on the lid. Pocket tinder boxes (of which in some cases the edges formed the steel) were also fashionable. The flint and the steel method gave rise to the flintlock pistol or gun and early in the eighteenth century this resulted in the pistol tinder box.

Even as late as the writer's childhood days the rushlight was a common illuminant in the houses of the Welsh uplands. The common soft rush was the most suitable for the purpose. The rushes were gathered in summer, the longest and largest being selected. The whole of the peel was removed with the exception of a narrow rib running from one end of the rush to the other: this was left as a 'backbone' for the pith. The rushes were then drawn through hot melted fat held in a long narrow pan called a gresset and then left to harden. They were then ready for use. They could be used as tapers in the hand or placed in a rushlight holder. The most primitive type of holder was the split stick placed in a small baseboard, the rush being placed diagonally through the cleft and moved forward periodically as it burned.

The common rushlight holder however was pincer-type, of iron with a wooden or iron base (Plate 35). These were always the products of the local blacksmith's craft. The movable side of the pincer sometimes ended in a knob but often in a sconce for a tallow candle so that both rushlight and candle could be used together when required. These objects are beautiful in their simplicity and often illustrate smithcraft at its best. Hanging rushlights also were commonly found in farmhouse and cottage, often suspended from a horizontal iron bar fixed in the breastsummer of the fire-place and along which it could be moved to suit the occupants of the fireside seats.

Primitive as was the rushlight it was probably not the earliest method of illumination in Europe. This was probably the fir-candle, a splinter of resinous wood, the *lluch bin* of sixth-century Welsh poetry, and much used too as one would expect in the pine-forested Scottish Highlands. In Ireland as in Scotland they were often made of bog fir.

Tallow candles were used in the Middle Ages and continued to be made down to the nineteenth century. The simplest way of making these was to take narrow bands of linen, tying about six or eight of them to a wooden rod and then dipping their lengths in a vat of boiling tallow. The process was repeated many times until the tallowed strip had attained the proportions of a candle. Indeed a rush was occasionally used as a wick but it shed such a dismal light, 'darkness visible' in Gilbert White's phrase, that the rag wick was generally preferred. The great fault of these candles was that the wick as it burned remained in the flame and obstructed, indeed often extinguished, it. It needed therefore constantly to be trimmed or snuffed. Snuffers for this purpose were made as early as the fifteenth century and by the eighteenth and early nineteenth centuries had become dainty objects of silver, steel, brass or of Sheffield plate. During the nineteenth century the plaited wick, a French invention, was introduced. The method of plaiting caused the wick as it burned to curve away from the flame so making snuffing unnecessary. The plaited wick continues to be used.

In the eighteenth and nineteenth centuries, tinned iron candle-moulds, in which the wicks were placed and the tallow poured in, became common.

In the nineteenth century ordinary paraffin lamps became more and more fashionable throughout the countryside. But the country custom of going to bed with the approach of darkness and the use of rushlights and candles hindered the introduction of more sophisticated forms of artificial lighting, until the First World War changed social conditions completely.

LAUNDERING

Washing and preparing linen were always domestic tasks of importance. The hand mangle-board consisting of a stout board with a handle fixed like a plane-handle, and a roller, is a type widespread throughout Europe. The top surface of the board lent itself to such decoration as chip carving and other ornamentation, the handle often being carved with zoomorphic designs. Some of the more elaborately ornamented Scandinavian mangle-boards are notable. In Britain however, such boards appear to be of simple form without ornamentation, the handle being a plain cylindrical extension at one end giving the board the semblance of a cricket bat. Such examples are known in Wales.

This simple device, generally used on a table, was developed towards the end of the eighteenth century and became popular in the countryside in Victorian times. It was now a ponderous box mangle with its huge chest weighted with stones. The chest was moved to and fro on free rollers, by turning a handle. In several parts of Wales the farming communities seem to have adopted this somewhat clumsy attempt at the mechanization of a laborious domestic chore.

For smoothing linen, glass calenders were used but the box-iron became popular in the eighteenth century. This had an iron heater —a solid triangle of iron which was placed in the fire for heating: this was inserted through a door at the larger end of the box. The box-irons stood upon three-legged stands, of iron or brass. Various forms were introduced during the nineteenth century.

For preparing ruffles, flounces and frills, a special implement was used. It was called a goffering or tally iron, tally being a corruption of 'Italian iron' after the country from which these irons were introduced early in the seventeenth century. During the following century they were made in a variety of designs and metals or combinations of metals. These irons consisted of a bar similar in form to a poker which when red-hot was placed into an iron 'barrel' which it fitted so heating the barrel. The starched linen was grasped in both hands and placed over the hot barrel which made a semi-circular crimp. The process was repeated until the ruffle, flounce or frill was fully crimped.

There was another type of gofferer particularly popular in Wales. This was the wooden goffering frame (Plate 36). It consisted of two uprights, six inches or more apart, fixed into a stand, generally with a drawer below. The uprights were grooved on the inside to hold a stack of 'quills', thin rods of wood. A cross-piece above the quills was so arranged as to slide up and down the uprights. Both quills and cross-piece were removed and the end of the starched fabric laid on the stand. A quill was then dropped into place over it. The fabric was turned over the quill and another quill dropped over it. The remaining quills, twenty or more according to the length of the fabric, were treated in the same way, the fabric running in and out between them. The cross-piece was finally clamped down on the completed stack of quills and securely wedged in position. The whole gofferer was then placed near the fire and when the fabric was dry, it was removed fully crimped. This was a safer method of goffering than that of using the red-hot tally iron.

Crimping boards were also used. These were grooved boards with a similarly grooved wooden roller worked upon it. A nineteenth-century development of this was the miniature mangle type, consisting of two fluted metal rollers juxtaposed horizontally in a frame similar to that of the larger clothes mangle and turned by means of a handle. The fabric was inserted between the rollers which were hollow and open at one end so that they could be heated by the insertion of small goffering irons.

Laundering in Britain although carried out by the household staffs of country mansions and farmhouses was also a cottage industry and much work was 'farmed out' to cottage women who thus supplemented their husbands' meagre earnings.

Chapter 4

Costume

'Society' declared the philosopher of clothes, 'is founded upon Cloth' which often transforms the human body into something rich and strange. This belief may be hyperbole but it holds an important element of truth. Clothes are now more dependent upon fashion than is any other aspect of folk life. The origins of changes of fashion, often elusive, in clothes have been summarized by Miss Thalassa Cruso[1] under five headings, namely the influence of individuals, the influence of public opinion, foreign influence, the influence of dress-makers and manufacturers, and the influence of war and trade.

The influence of individuals is well illustrated in the matter of so-called national costumes. England, with its national status secure in its powerful political state, has never boasted of a national costume. Her Keltic neighbours, Scotland and Wales, have been less fortunate. The urge in these unfortunately stateless countries to assert their national identity has caused many Scots and Welshmen to speak glibly and to write freely of traditional kilts and tartans, bedgowns and tall hats. The dress of a large part of Scotland for a considerable period was the belted plaid. To be dogmatic about how this was worn before the end of the seventeenth century, much more evidence is required. 'If one thinks in how many different ways a lady can wear a shawl, it will be appreciated what even a mere man could do with some ten yards of hard-wearing woollen cloth which was part of his dress by day and his blanket at night . . . When the plaid was cut in two, resulting in the waist-to-knee kilt as we have it today, is not known'.[2] H. F.

[1] In *Costume*, London Museum Catalogue No. 5, 1934, pp. 15–21.

[2] Stuart Maxwell and Robin Hutchison: *Scottish Costume 1550–1850*, London, 1958, p. 156.

McClintock, in his scholarly work on Highland dress,[1] dismisses the belief that 'the kilt is of remote antiquity in Scotland' and also that 'it has been the national dress from time immemorial'. His personal belief is that Chief Ian MacDonell (along with an Englishman named Thomas Rawlinson in the eighteenth century) may be regarded as 'the father of the modern kilt'. It was in the nineteenth century that the round brooch, 'with the addition of a central cairngorm became during the Highland dress revival . . . the shoulder fastening for the plaid'. In the same century it was 'a combination of military and Victorian modesty which gave birth to the ungainly long, mid-nineteenth-century civilian, and current Army kilt. The Army is also responsible for perpetuating the monstrous horsehair sporrans with shaving-brush tassels.'[2] The sporran was a leather purse (with a thong as a draw string) which was looped over the belt. This attractive dress accessory descended in aesthetic quality as well as in position as the modern kilt evolved.

It becomes obvious therefore that the kilt is a late element in Highland dress, that it is in no sense part of a traditional Scottish costume, and that it came into being through the intervention of an individual Englishman. In the same way McClintock (op. cit., p. 98) states that in the sixteenth century the kilt 'did not exist' in Ireland, and adduces evidence to show that it did not exist before or after that period. He suggests that the theory of its existence 'originated with O'Curry in the middle of the nineteenth century'. When these facts are considered, it appears all the more absurd that there should exist in Wales in recent years a small band of misguided folk who attempt to 'revive' (as part of a non-existent 'national dress') a Welsh kilt!

The story of the 'traditional Welsh costume' also shows the influence of individuals. Mr. Ffransis G. Payne[3] has described how there was a period when a widespread contemporary fashion found in many countries in Europe developed in Wales, as elsewhere, local characteristics of material and perhaps colour, within a rural

[1] H. F. McClintock: *Old Irish and Highland Dress*, Dundalk, 1943, pp. 141–2.

[2] Maxwell and Hutchison: op. cit., p. 158.

[3] Ffransis G. Payne: 'Welsh Peasant Costume', in *Folk Life* II, 1964, pp. 42–57. Also issued as a separate publication by the Welsh Folk Museum.

20. A dug-out chest, medieval, from Llanbryn-Mair parish church, Montgomeryshire (in the Welsh Folk Museum)

21. Ark-lid chest, Llantrisant, Glamorgan (in the Welsh Folk Museum)

22. Dower chest, 17th century with later front panel, from Monmouthshire (in the Welsh Folk Museum)

23. Panelled chair from Pembrokeshire. Early 16th century (in the Welsh Folk Museum)

24. Chair (in the National Library of Wales MS. Peniarth 28), 12th century

25. 'Justice's Chair', Tregib, Carmarthenshire, 16th century (in the Welsh Folk Museum)

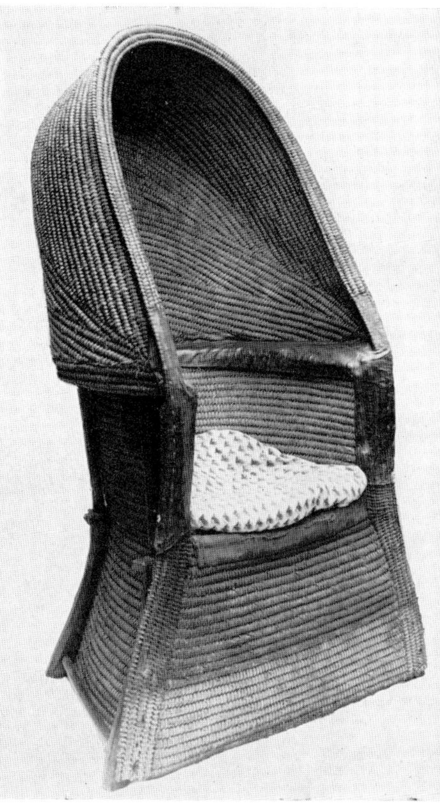

26. Lip-work chair (in the Welsh Folk Museum)

27. Fireside cupboard-bed, Kennixton, Gower (in the Welsh Folk Museum)

28. Detail of bed-head, in Cilewent, Radnorshire (in the Welsh Folk Museum)

29. Press cupboard from Cardiganshire. Late 18th century (in the Welsh Folk Museum)

society. This was followed by a period 'of natural change and deterioration in a society that was itself beginning to disintegrate. During this period some people desired to retain an "ideal" unchanging Welsh costume and consider it a *national* costume.' This was the period beginning about 1830. In 1836 Lady Llanover, a romantic English lady who became well-known as a fervent Welsh nationalist and pan-Kelticist, published an essay on the 'preservation of the Welsh language and national costumes of Wales'. Her prime purpose was to consolidate and expand the Welsh woollen industry and to spurn all foreign cottons and similar light materials. She painted water-colours of the costumes of country women whom she saw in different parts of south Wales and offered prizes at *eisteddfodau* for 'national checks and stripes' and even for beaver hats.

As Payne suggests she 'lost the battle for flannel and wool alone but . . . she turned farm servants' working clothes into a conscious, or rather self-conscious national costume.' There is no evidence for believing that the combination of bedgown, petticoat and tall beaver hat was at any time a Welsh national costume. Payne's 'final period', as he states, 'is still with us. The old country dress is re-created as a fancy dress for special occasions. And recreated from the imaginary creations of postcard and souvenir merchants, the sort of thing possible only in a society that has lost its real roots.' This is fair criticism, for as the kilt appears to be most popular amongst marginal non-Gaelic speaking Scotsmen, and the largest leeks worn at an international rugby football match by non-Welsh-speaking 'Welshmen', so the fancy Welsh 'national costume' is favoured only by those on the fringes of Welsh nationality.

Although Lady Llanover evolved 'a weird and wonderful' costume for her domestic harpist she was not concerned with a national costume for men. As a result no national dress for men has ever been mentioned, and the recent absurd suggestion that a 'Welsh kilt' should be used is an attempt to create such a costume!

The history of English costume, as that of Scottish and Irish dress, has been the subject of many specialist studies but the history of Welsh dress has yet to be written. There are references in the early poetry, some of which takes us back to the sixth century, to silk clothing, to mantles, and to *brithwe*, possibly a many-coloured cloth; to red and purple dresses, to brooches, chaplets, gold torques and amber beads. In a fascinating poem, a small boy's dress is called a *pais* ('petticoat' in modern usage) and it was made from the skins of pine-martens. In the early medieval period, the tales of the Mabinogion have dazzling descriptions, e.g. a maiden dressed in a silk vest with clasps of gold, a surcoat of gold tissue, a frontlet of gold upon her head with rubies, gems and pearls. These were obviously instances of royal apparel. The horseman, in the story of Pwyll, prince of Dyfed, 'clad in garments of grey woollen', must have been a more ordinary sight.

Much could be written about elements in dress which have remained after outliving their purpose and usefulness, e.g. the buttons on the sleeve of a man's jacket, the remains of the fashionable cuff of two hundred years ago. Other elements in dress such as the fantastic cracowes, the long pointed shoes fashionable in the fourteenth century, have long disappeared but not before enriching our language. The toes of these shoes were tightly stuffed with hay, giving rise to the saying still occasionally to be met with in the countryside that a wealthy person is he who has hay in his shoes. To trace these elements would however involve us in a history of costume well beyond the scope of this volume.

Another instance of the influence of individuals and of 'learned' movements on costume is illuminating and merits a reference here. The antiquarian movement of the eighteenth century, led by such figures as William Stukeley,[1] found adherents in Wales, notably Edward Williams (1747–1826), generally known by his bardic title Iolo Morganwg. These men spread the belief that Welsh bardism was descended from the Druids, and Iolo, who was a complex mixture of brilliant scholar and literary forger (he was a stonemason by trade), declared that the bards of his native Glamorgan had secretly maintained the old druidic tradition throughout the ages, producing manuscript evidence of his own skilful forging to 'prove' his contention. As a result he created an institution which he called the Gorsedd of the Bards of the Isle of Britain, holding its

[1] Stuart Piggott: *William Stukeley*, Oxford, 1950.

first druidic ceremony in 1791 on Primrose Hill in London, thus capturing the most important London Welshmen of his day and obtaining publicity in such journals as *The Gentleman's Magazine*.

Iolo and his Gorsedd were however suspect since he was an avowed supporter of the French Revolutionaries and a radical thinker. His Gorsedd seemed likely to die an early death. His next step to save it revealed his genius. The Cambrian Society of Dyfed was to hold an eisteddfod in Carmarthen in 1819: it was to be a three-day festival. On the Saturday following this festival, in the garden of the Ivy Bush Hotel in Carmarthen, Iolo held a Gorsedd ceremony. He marked out the bardic circle and the 'logan stone' with pebbles carried on his person and the druids, bards and ovates —the three orders of the Gorsedd—were invested with ribbons, white, blue and green, tied on their right arms. By such means, this counterfeit institution was grafted on to the traditional eisteddfod. Before the end of the nineteenth century, the pebbles had grown into massive stone circles and the arm ribbons into the flowing white, blue and green robes designed—such was the irony of the situation—by Hubert von Herkomer. The Gorsedd, far from remaining an unimportant appendix to the eisteddfod, now insinuated itself into the festival itself, claiming the right to crown the poet and chair the winning bard in full panoply, on two separate days. All its members have become *ex officio* members of the governing body of the National Eisteddfod. The meetings of the robed members of the Gorsedd are now looked upon as part of the festival's pageantry; this spurious antiquarianism is considered by the uninformed to be the traditional eisteddfod. It is a classic example of the influence of a dedicated individual on costume and ceremony.

The influence of public opinion upon fashion is generally not creative but tends to be censorious. The short-lived topless dresses of recent years were quickly abandoned because they offended what was held to be public decency. The harsh morality of the Commonwealth period caused the gay fashions of the court of the first Charles to be abandoned for a greatly simplified fashion which disappeared completely with the Restoration.

Foreign influence is well illustrated in Britain by the long dominance of Paris and of French fashions for a period of nearly a thousand years. The Norman conquest imposed a French aristocracy upon England and French fashions have remained in considerable degree the 'aristocratic' fashions particularly for women. The French Revolution broke the tradition for a time, and following it men's fashions became based on London models.

The influence of coutouriers and dressmakers is in many ways a modern development which still maintains its importance, the great fashion designers of Paris issuing their new designs regularly. The copying of these designs at cheap rates has helped to remove the distinctions which formerly existed between the 'aristocracy' and the common folk. This development illustrates the influence of the manufacturers but it also caused quick changes in dress fashions.

War, trade and industry have done much to influence fashions in dress. For example, during the two world wars of 1914–18 and 1939–45, when women worked in factories and were attached to the armed forces, utilitarian fashions in dress were introduced. Most of the elements remained in the fashions of the succeeding years. Trade in such materials as India muslins and furs had a profound effect upon fashions in Europe. In recent years the industrial production of nylon and artificial materials has greatly changed fashions in dress.

But throughout the centuries until recent times, fashion in dress was the concern of the wealthier members of the community; it was from their social circles that one found individuals who slavishly 'followed' each fashion as it appeared. The country folk—and indeed the urban workers—disregarded the fashions of the day, continuing to dress in clothes which were useful and hard-wearing.

Cunnington[1] has summed up the fundamental change in dress fashions when he writes of them as 'spreading over a far wider social field than formerly, so that ultimately only the poorest section of the community remains unaffected. Fashion has now become a democratic expression instead of being, as it once was, the exclusive symbol of the upper class outlook.'

[1] C. Willett Cunnington: *English Women's Clothing in the Present Century*, London, 1952, p. 19.

Chapter 5

Aspects of Social Life

The social life of many European nations has been studied from several angles. The student of folk life however is concerned with the individual as a whole, in his 'actual manner of living'[1] both as an individual personality and as an individual in society. His approach has to be more complete and all-round than that of the sociologist or the student of pure geography. He must take into consideration 'the individual himself and his oral or written evidence, as well as his instruments, his products, and the actual traces of his activities in nature'.[1] Erixon, following Henry J. Burt, holds that to say how a group behaves is 'merely description; it is neither analysis nor explanation'. The analysis and explanation are found only by dealing with the functions and reactions of individual members of the group. It is true however that the family is more than a group: it is a unit, functioning economically and to an extent socially 'under the leadership of the master of the house' and there have been instances —although this has become less true in modern times—where the village was, to quote Erixon again, 'a company for the safeguard of the families' common interests and for their collaboration'. We are concerned with such units, but also with much more—the analysis of human functions, the study of persons. The approach of the economist and the sociologist is, in this sense, incomplete and can indeed result in dangerous misconceptions.

We have already written of some elements from the past which have survived into the present. A distinguished anthropologist, the late R. R. Marrett, in a presidential address[2] in 1914 to the Folklore

[1] Sigurd Erixon: 'Regional European Ethnology, II', in *Folk-Liv*, 1938, p. 263.

[2] R. R. Marrett: 'Folklore and Psychology', in *Folk-Lore*, XXV, 1914, pp. 12–33.

Society of London, posed the question, why do survivals survive? Here we are confronted with two views of the study of man and society, the one seeing survivals important in the same sense that fossils and human artefacts are important; the other emphasizing the way in which the conditions of social life actively encourage survivals. These two views—the historical and the sociological—have been presented, attacked and defended by numerous writers. Neither view presents the complete truth. Antiquarianism, in Marrett's words, 'may easily be overdone'. On the other hand, sociological and, in particular, economic studies can present a dangerously incomplete picture. To the study of the social body must be added a 'study of the soul', if the study is to be complete. It is this kind of integrated study with which we are concerned.

'Societies', wrote Herbert Spencer, 'are aggregates which grow.' But they grow in every age on foundations provided by the human mind: these are eternal in the human spirit—love and hate, generosity and greed, tolerance and prejudice, religion and superstition, and much else. It has been well said by Arthur Mitchell[1] that 'evil does not cease to be evil though it is spoken of in mild and polished phrases; and, in one sense, it matters little whether men go into battle with stone axes, bronze swords or iron guns. Are not the promptings to war still the same, and do not its spirit and its issues remain unchanged? . . . Is not the bloody business essentially the same in its nature, and the same too in its purposes in the hands of men who lay ambushes and carry off scalps as trophies, as it is in the hands of men who blow up forts by secret mining or ships by skulking torpedoes? . . . Ought we not to recognize in war one of the many threads which run all through our high civilization and connect it with that savagery of which we proudly but ignorantly boast that we bear no trace?'

The 'many threads which run all through' our civilization—this is the fundamental truth. The greater part of our lives is made up of 'survivals': in this sense, all tradition is survival. But thus to express the problem is to oversimplify it. The eighteenth-century notion of Progress, of 'Man, according to the philosophers and rationalists, . . . climbing steadily out of the mire of superstition,

[1] op. cit., pp. 193–4.

ignorance, savagery, into a world that was to become ever more polished, humane and rational—the world of the Paris salons before the hailstorm of revolution broke the window-panes and drove the talkers to the cellar'[1]—is seen to be no longer true. There have been great recessions, as well as advances, in human development. The standards of scientific thought and achievement are probably higher in the twentieth century than at any other time in history. But no other century has seen so many intensive upthrusts into barbarism and savagery: the technological leap was not accompanied by the spiritual leap. Society has to face the fact of change and accumulation, but human life remains and spiritual values are ever fundamental. This is the factor, which in periods of recession such as the present, is always overlooked, and to our cost ignored. The fact of change, too, is significant: for instance, superstition remains but in many new forms as well as maintaining some of the old. Institutions decay but new kinds emerge. But the tyranny of economics and technology at the expense of the spiritual expansion and enrichment of life may yet cause the ultimate irrevocable disaster, the annihilation of man.

* * *

These thoughts are an essential prelude to a brief survey of social life in the non-industrial communities of parts of Britain—one of the richest fields of folk-life study. The discussion in this chapter is concerned mainly with Wales (see also Introduction). One can write with real meaning only of a society well known to the author: to attempt a comparative study of various societies without intimate experience and knowledge of each would be meaningless and misleading. Giraldus Cambrensis (Gerald of Wales), writing in the twelfth century his description of Wales, based on the knowledge he had gained on his itinerary of Wales with Archbishop Baldwin in 1188, stated that the Welsh 'do not dwell together in either town or village or fort but, like hermits, remain in the woods. And their custom on the edge of the forests is not to build large mansions or fine costly buildings of stone or brick, but to build huts of wattled

[1] Lewis Mumford: *Technics and Civilization*, London, 1946, p. 182.

rods to serve for a year . . . Their land is therefore mostly pasture, tilth is scarce'.[1]

Much of what Gerald found has been changed in the course of eight centuries but the Welsh never developed a tradition of town and village building. Many of the towns of Wales developed from Anglo-Norman garrisons or were initially English settlements. The industrial age produced the vast conurbations of south-east Wales, from Llanelli and Swansea to Cardiff and Newport with their industrial hinterland. Throughout the centuries however the Welsh lived in farmsteads scattered over the high moorlands or in the deep valleys and in cottages and small holdings clustered around the long Welsh coast-line. Small centres for trade and marketing developed as small towns or villages (e.g. Bala, Tregaron, Machynlleth, Llandeilo). These and their like became the focal points of local communities which were in most instances defined by the *cantref* boundaries of the Welsh Laws, boundaries often ignored in the creation of Welsh counties in the Act of Union with England in 1536. The local loyalties of pre-Union days have survived however to a remarkable degree even into the twentieth century, helped undoubtedly by the topographical configuration of the country. Until the coming of the motor-car and recent transport developments many of these small communities were considerably isolated and were the homes of close-knit communities, essentially self-supporting, literate, and culturally most active. Loyalty to *bro*, the 'region' of the small community, transcended any loyalty to Wales, a nation without a state or (until recently) a capital. To a native of, let us say, Montgomeryshire, the neighbouring town of Shrewsbury beyond the border, or indeed London itself, was far more real than Swansea or Cardiff in the far south or Caernarfon in the fastnesses of the inaccessible north. The only bond which tied these remote areas all together against the alluring east beyond the border was that of a common language which the Saxon made no attempt, out of duty, expediency, or courtesy, to master. No state bound all these separate communities together into a real self-conscious nation nor has any London government to this day agreed to the creation of a major road-complex which would provide

[1] Translated from Thomas Jones: *Gerallt Gymro*, Cardiff, 1938, p. 202.

ease of travel between the scattered communities of Wales: all major roads still run from west to east—Holyhead to London, Aberystwyth to London, Fishguard to London. No capital city in Europe is similar to Cardiff, the Welsh capital, where all its major roads run eastwards to Birmingham or London or westwards as far as Swansea but not northwards through the vast area of the Welsh-speaking communities. Topography and nature have been allowed to dominate the Welsh social body, even in an age when man reaches for the moon. Some economists and politicians are so bemused by the idea of maintaining the east-west relationship of the island of Britain, set up in the sixteenth century, that they have even pressed for the solution of the problem of the rural depopulation of central Wales by using it as an overspill area for the English Midlands and the creation there of new conurbations. They do not seem to realize that the unification of Wales through the making of north-south roads, electrification, piped water etc. would revive both her culture and her economy.

★ ★ ★

There are many facets to the life of an ordered society, e.g. weights and measures, money, law and order, folk medicine and practices, superstition and religion. In a rural society, units of measurement were often determined with reference to average lengths of the distances between hand and elbow or thumb and little finger. 'Three fingers thick' is a measurement recorded in the Welsh Laws. In the same way, the width of the thumb was a standard unit of measurement. There were several such units and, indeed, several variations, even in the length of the 'yardstick' which could differ by as much as a foot from country to country. One could find the yard, the 'yard and handful' (called the forty-inch ell), the 'yard and inch', also known as the Scotch ell and generally used as a cloth measure. These were standardized in the eighteenth and nineteenth centuries by such acts of Parliament as those of 1758–60, 1824 and 1878. Despite legal standardization, rural custom maintained some of the traditional measures well into the twentieth century.

In the same way, the 'Winchester Bushel' and 'ale gallon' of

Henry VII became well known as did the 'choppin' or half pint of 1555 in Scotland. In Wales the 'wool pound'—a stone weight—was the unit used for weighing butter, yarn, flannel, cheese, tallow and most of the necessities of daily life. Only very slowly did the rural communities, in particular, come to adopt the legal standards ordained by Parliament.

The growth of cattle-droving between Wales and the London area and the beginning of the industrial revolution helped to revolutionize methods of finance in the countryside and towns. The development of mining (lead, copper and coal) and of the woollen industry, as well as commercial ventures generally, necessitated the payment of weekly wages to growing numbers of employees, although barter still continued as a recognized method of business. In the eighteenth century however as the financial basis of social life began to alter, the change was met in two ways, by the issue of paper and metal tokens and by the formation of local banks.

Tokens were principally related to early industry; a wool factory in Montgomeryshire, the Parys Mountain Copper Company in Anglesey, the Flint Lead Works, and various industries in Carmarthenshire, Glamorgan and Monmouthshire all produced token coins which were payable locally and often (as in the case of the Anglesey coins), 'on demand in London, Liverpool, or Anglesey'. In the industrial valleys of south Wales, this coinage became so well known as to give a new word to the local Welsh dialects, *tocyns* (from 'tokens') for 'pennies'. Token money was prohibited by Act of Parliament in 1817.

Rich drovers were the founders of the first banks in Wales. Returning from their journeys to London with considerable amounts of money, nothing was more natural than that they should lend it at interest. So began *Banc y Ddafad Ddu* (the Black Sheep Bank) of Messrs. Evans, Jones and Davies at Aberystwyth and Tregaron about 1800. A pound note bore a representation of one sheep, two on a two-pounds note, and a lamb on a ten-shilling note. This was for easy recognition by countrymen not used to much reading. The 'Ship Bank' (*Banc y Llong*) had been established in Aberystwyth in 1762. Llandovery in Carmarthenshire followed in 1799 with *Banc yr Eidion Du* ('the Bank of the Black Bullock'). These local banks multiplied: in Wales they were found at Llanelli, Tenby, Haverfordwest, Milford Haven, Brecon, Crickhowell, Presteigne, Swansea, Cardiff, Newport, Wrexham, Newtown, Llanidloes, Welshpool, Dolgellau and other country towns. In time most of them were absorbed into larger banks so that by the end of the nineteenth century, the great London banks appeared in all these small Welsh towns.

In the eighteenth century and the early years of the following century, the clipping and grinding of gold coins caused much trouble in business circles. This illegal practice was finally prevented by the introduction of milled edges. Until this was done, balances to test and weigh gold money were used. The inventive genius of their manufacturers produced a variety of types, such as counter models for use in banks and trading houses, small steelyard types, pocket scales in oval japanned or rectangular wooden boxes, and special balances for guinea and half-guinea pieces. For a considerable period, varieties of these balances were in almost universal use and most folk collections in museums contain examples of them.

The maintenance of law and order was always of importance in social life. In the early Welsh Laws punishments for various crimes, offences and misdemeanours were clearly defined. In these laws, that relating to capital punishment was much more enlightened than in some neighbouring countries. The death penalty was confined to 'homicide, certain acts of theft, treason, and, according to some authorities, arson'.[1] Death was by hanging. Ellis writes that in the English law of that time 'provisions for death and mutilation [had] regulations absent from the Welsh law. The death penalty was common, and till Æthelstan's time it could be inflicted for the offence of "theft present" on any child of the age of twelve. Even his amendment, which raised the age to fifteen, did not apply to a fugitive, or one evading capture or one guilty of a second offence'. This continued to be the law till a late period.

In its 'provisions for mutilation' early English law revelled. Cnut, we are told, decreed 'gentle punishment' for 'Christian men'. By this was meant that anyone twice convicted was to have his hands or his feet or both cut off, 'according to the nature

[1] T. P. Ellis: op. cit., II, pp. 72, 76.

of his offence'. If he had 'wrought greater evil' his eyes could be put out, his ears and upper lips be cut off or he could be scalped.[1] This sacrificing of limbs was rare in Welsh law, nor could a youth under fourteen be executed. Tonsured clerks and necessitous thieves were also excluded from the death penalty for theft as were pregnant women and married women committed jointly with their husbands.

The savage punishments which had been long an English tradition gave rise to several 'refinements' of torture in Anglo-Saxon and medieval times (and indeed later). The practice of gibbeting or hanging in chains the body of the executed wrong-doer near the site of his crime was generally prevalent in order to deter others from committing such offences. There is evidence of this from the thirteenth and fourteenth centuries. It has even been asserted that some criminals were gibbeted alive. But it was not until 1752 (25 George II) that gibbeting was legally recognized: it was abolished by statute in 1834. Few complete gibbet irons survive. The body was left to disintegrate as did the irons in which it was placed. All that generally remained were the skull inside the gibbet 'cap' (Plate 37). Pressing to death by placing weights upon the prostrate offender whose arms and legs were first drawn apart and secured, was another inhumane method of punishment and of execution practised in England down to the eighteenth century—indeed until 1827. It is right to record too that even boiling to death was practised in London between 1531 and 1547.

The pillory, whipping post, stocks and ducking stool were instruments of punishment throughout the centuries; there were also finger pillories for holding the offender by the fingers, which must have been exceedingly painful. Stocks, in particular, have a long history dating to Anglo-Saxon times. Many towns had these for the official punishment of offenders, drunkenness being often the cause of such punishment. Even a small Welsh country town like Dolgellau had its movable stocks (Plate 38). Often the whipping post and stocks were placed close to each other and remained in use well into the nineteenth century. Andrews[2] records from a con-

[1] ibid., pp. 77–8.

[2] William Andrews: *Bygone Punishments*, London, 1899, p. 219.

stable's accounts in Huntingdonshire that in 1690–1 an insane woman was whipped at the post and in 1710–11 a certain person was paid 'for whipping 2 people y[t] had small-pox'.

Scolds—the term is applicable only to females—were offenders against the public peace and were punished in a variety of ways. The ducking stool, placed at the end of a horizontal balancing beam working on a vertical central post, was possibly the least inhumane of these. The offending female was placed in the chair which could be plunged into the nearby pool as often as the sentence directed 'to cool her immoderate heat'. The scold's bridle, or brank, was less humane. It consisted of an iron frame or 'cage' placed over the head, a band of iron with a locking device encircling the head at mouth level. In the front there was a flat iron plate, sharpened or covered with spikes, which projected into the offender's mouth holding down the tongue (Plate 39). Any movement of the tongue could result in injury. The scold was led through the town or village by a chain holding this 'bridle' and often left tied to the whipping post.

Local communities however had their own methods of punishing or holding up to ridicule those who offended against their society. For example, in the village of Cynwyl Elfed in Carmarthenshire there used to be a huge oak tree in the village square, and below the tree a white stone (*Y Garreg Wen*). This was for generations the village meeting place and under this tree offenders against the moral laws of the community were tried. When a person had so offended, a large effigy of him was prepared and placed high on the white stone in view of the crowd which formed 'the people's court'. A man who had climbed to the topmost branches of the tree was the Judge or the Voice from Above, and below, near the effigy, the Prosecutor. When the audience had encircled the effigy, a dialogue ensued between judge and prosecutor. The prosecutor would shout: 'Who has sinned?' to be answered by the Voice from Above: 'So-and-so' (naming the culprit). The offence was then named—immorality, theft, drunkenness etc.—and the evidence given. Finally came the verdict of 'guilty' and the people asked to consider a suitable punishment. This was invariably to suspend the effigy from the tree and then to burn it, which was accomplished 'with dignity and devotion'.

People's courts performed other functions of social justice: they showed the society's displeasure towards errant wives or husbands or indeed quarrelsome couples or persons guilty of immoral practices: this was done by making the person ridiculed the laughing stock of the community. Such judgements were more effective than the 'due processes' of law for in closely-knit communities ridicule could be extremely effective. These 'Courts' had a wide distribution. In parts of Scotland and the north of England they were known as 'Riding the Stang'; in south-west England, 'Skimmington' or 'Skimmety'; in various parts of Wales, *cwltrin* or *cwlstrin* or *y ceffyl pren* (the wooden horse). One of the fundamentals of this 'court' was charivari or a medley of sounds, 'rough music' as it has been termed. T. Gwynn Jones has described the Welsh *cwltrin*:[1]

'It was a noisy procession that proceeded to the house of a henpecked husband, near which a Court was formed, the Judge wearing the collar-bone of a horse on his head and a bed quilt over his shoulders, and the officers carrying long white wands. Husband and wife were impersonated, the male carrying a broom and the female a ladle. If found guilty, especially of drawing blood, the representative of the wife was carried on the wooden horse through the village. Two standards were borne, a petticoat and a pair of breeches, on poles. The petticoat was placed in front of the culprits' house and pelted with addled eggs and other missiles, the breeches were elevated, and the punishment ended.'

This custom was found, with many local variations, throughout Wales, down to the end of the nineteenth century. Isolated examples as at Tregaron in Cardiganshire occurred as late as the nineteen-twenties.[2] Its frequent appearance in Glamorgan is attested by the excellent descriptions given by contemporary observers.[3] Under the name 'skimity', it was 'still by no means infrequent' in west

[1] T. Gwynn Jones: *Welsh Folklore and Folk Custom*, London, 1930, p. 191.

[2] Trefor M. Owen: *Welsh Folk Customs*, Cardiff, 1959, p. 172.

[3] See, for instance, G. J. Williams: 'Glamorgan Customs in the eighteenth century', in *Gwerin*, I, 1956, 106–8.

Somersetshire in the early years of the present century.[1] Examples are also cited by Wright from Yorkshire, Worcestershire, Kent, Hampshire, Wiltshire, Dorset and Devon.

An important person in the life of the countryside has been for many generations the family doctor—important if only because he had many opportunities of intimate knowledge of the people whom he served: he came to know not only their physical ailments but also their thoughts and minds, the urges which drove them sometimes to strange actions and the hopes and faith which maintained them in a hard and often unsympathetic world. Occasionally one meets a country doctor who has recorded his experiences: such records provide vitally important material for the student of folk life for they throw light, to use Erixon's expression, on 'the soul' of the individual in society.

There has been a long tradition of medicine in certain parts of Wales. The physicians of Myddfai (*meddygon Myddfai*) in Carmarthenshire were reputed to be descended from the fairy lady of the lake (*Llyn y Fan Fach*) who when she appeared out of the waters of the lake was courted by a local farmer who married her on her one condition that he should never strike her thrice. The farmer, his family and his farm at Esgair Llaethdy in Myddfai prospered exceedingly until, accidentally, the poor man touched his wife on the shoulder thrice. She and her animals disappeared immediately into the lake whence she had come. The legend is internationally known and may be explained only as an important element in folk memory. This we are not now concerned with, but it is an interesting gloss on this internationally known tale that in Wales the physicians of Myddfai were reputed to be the sons of this marriage, the mother having told her eldest son 'that his mission on earth was to be a benefactor to mankind by relieving them from pain and misery, through healing all manner of their diseases; for which purpose she furnished him with a bag full of medicinal prescriptions'.[2] There are farms in the parish known as *Llwyn Ifan Feddyg* (the grove of Ifan the physician) and *Llwyn Meredydd Feddyg* (the grove of Meredydd

[1] Joseph Wright: *The English Dialect Dictionary*, London, 1904, s.v. 'skimmington'.

[2] Sir John Rhŷs: *Celtic Folklore*, Oxford, 1901, p. 11.

the physician) and down to the middle of the eighteenth century, physicians were known to flourish in the Myddfai area. Descendants of the physicians were known as eminent physicians down to recent times. The manuscript of what may be termed 'a bag full of medicinal prescriptions' dates from the fifteenth century.

The 'conjurer' or medicine-man, known in Wales as the *dyn hysbys* (wizard or soothsayer), has been through the centuries an important figure in the rural society. This is certainly true of Wales. In a few instances, such as John Dee (1527–1608) of London, a graduate of Cambridge and fellow of Trinity College, Welshmen attained considerable eminence as 'conjurers of spirits'. The tradition still dies hard in some rural communities. One *dyn hysbys* in the Llangurig district of Montgomeryshire practised his 'art' until his recent death and was consulted by country men and women from an area extending many miles from his home. For example, a farmer had had a tooth extracted and could not stop the flow of blood. He was taken to the 'conjurer's' parlour and made to stand in the centre of the room where a circle in chalk was drawn around him. The 'conjurer' walked along this line uttering words which the farmer did not understand. 'The blood has been stopped,' he exclaimed to the farmer. 'No,' was the reply. 'Oh,' said the 'conjurer', 'I must walk in the reverse direction against the sun.' This he did for half an hour, and the blood ceased to flow.

Remedies and charms used in dealing with animals were often used by these men. A farmer would tell the *dyn hysbys* that his animals were dying. In due course, after consulting his books, the 'conjurer' would state that a neighbour had bewitched them and so affected the animals. He would then write on a piece of paper which he placed in a bottle which he sealed with lead. This bottle he ordered to be placed in the cowhouse, the stable or the pigsty under the roof or on the wallplate. One farmer stated some years ago that he had such bottles in each of his outhouses and would never dare to remove them since they ensured the health of all his stock. Difficulty in churning butter was removed by means of similar written charms placed near the churn (Plate 40).

Belief in bewitchment has survived the centuries and remains to this day. A few examples communicated to me by various medical

30. Piggin with interlocking band (in the Welsh Folk Museum)

1. Knocker churns and (centre) a hand-swinging churn (in the Welsh Folk Museum)

32. Rocking churn (in the Welsh Folk Museum)

33. Dog-driven box churn (in the Welsh Folk Museum)

34. Cheese press with box for stone weights and windlass action (in the Welsh Folk Museum)

36. Goffering frame (in the Welsh Folk Museum)

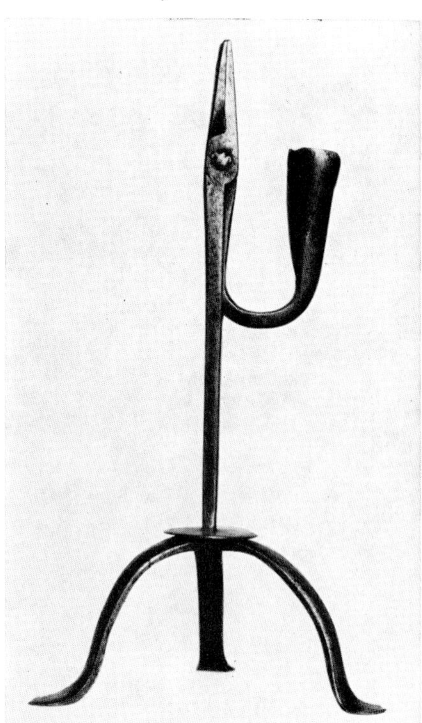

35. A rushlight and tallow-candle holder (in the Welsh Folk Museum)

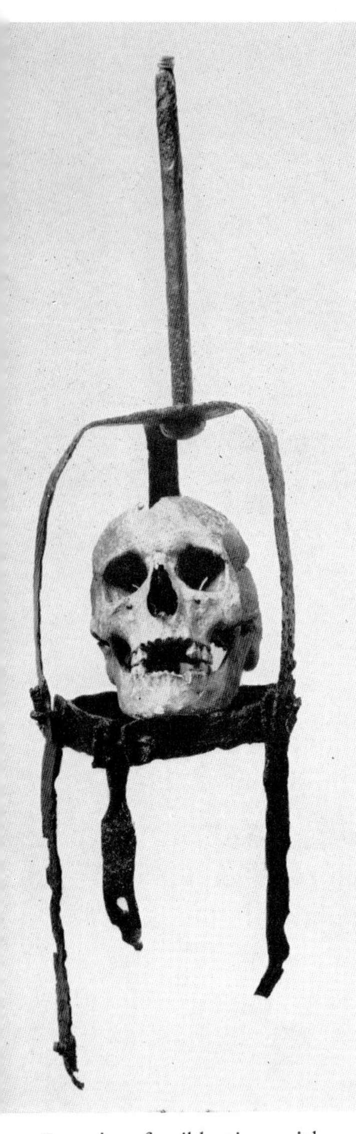

7. Remains of a gibbet iron with skull. From Dylife, Montgomeryshire (in the Welsh Folk Museum)

38. The town of Dolgellau (Merioneth) movable stocks (in the Welsh Folk Museum)

39. Scold's bridle or brank (in the Welsh Folk Museum)

40. 'Conjurer's' charm, Montgomeryshire. About 1916 (in the Welsh Folk Museum)

men are of interest. Such beliefs and practices are to be found in various forms throughout Britain and Ireland. For instance, in Wiltshire the devil is kept away from the farm stock by slitting the ears of the cows on Good Friday morning, always using a brand-new razor for the operation.

Some years ago on a mid-Wales farm, a large number of animals—sheep, pigs, geese and ducks—died. Geese and hens rushed to and fro in the farmyard, dropping dead. Things came to a pretty pass when the pony was found dead on top of the threshing machine. The 'conjurer' was sent for. He removed the pony's heart, took a steel rod, heated it and pushed it through the heart, lengthways and across to make the sign of the cross. Peace then prevailed in that farmyard.

When horses are bewitched and refuse to get up, and the veterinary surgeon has failed to discover any ailment or disease, the 'conjurer' is sent for. He pronounces thus: 'You will meet the man who has bewitched your horse: you will meet him on the village bridge. Ask him to come to the stable to bless the horse.' The farmer goes to the village, finds a man on the bridge (a popular meeting-place), insists on taking him to the stable and begs him to draw his hand over the horse from head to tail, saying: 'I will give thee my blessing.' The horse then stands up.

Even hens have to be dealt with circumspectly. An old man leaving his work at midday to walk home a distance of one and a half miles was asked where he was going. 'Home', he replied, 'to put the hen to sit on her eggs.' 'But your wife can do that.' 'No, no', was the reply, 'she doesn't know the proper words to tell the hen, and a hen will not hatch her eggs well if I do not place her on her nest and say the right words to her.' This is a widespread belief, for hens like cows and bees were part of the community.

The late Dr. Walter Davies of Llanidloes, Montgomeryshire, who told me of several of these occurrences, mentioned a case in which he had been called to see a child a piece of whose lip had been bitten off by a vicious dog. When he reached the farmhouse, he met the farmer who asked him what he wanted. When he told him that he had been called in by his wife, the mother, the farmer replied: 'She had no right to call you. I have been to see the conjurer and he told me to take some of the hairs of the dog which bit my child, mix them with lard and place the plaster on the lip. This I have done and you are not wanted.' Nor indeed was the doctor allowed to see the child, but he added wryly that when he left he noticed that the dog looked 'as if a hungry cow had been grazing on its back'.

Human beings were constantly being bewitched. An eminent Cardiganshire doctor told me of a patient, depressed and melancholy, whom he had treated regularly for a considerable time. Suddenly he ceased attending at the surgery and when next he saw him, he was in the best of health. In answer to the doctor's question, the man informed him that he had called in the 'conjurer', who had given the patient a description of the person who had bewitched him: with that knowledge the man was cured. 'Well,' said the doctor, 'I could have given you that description' and to the patient's astonishment, gave him a detailed description of the bewitcher. The countryman was most impressed for the description tallied exactly with that given by the 'conjurer'. 'How did you know?' he asked. 'Well,' said the doctor, 'if you look at yourself tonight in the mirror, you will see him for yourself.'

* * *

The examples quoted above help to prove that even in a literate community of considerable culture, such as that of the Welsh countryman, old superstitions die hard. At the same time, in the most sophisticated society, modern superstitions abound. The modern folklore of the motor-car is extensive while the ritual which the public of the 1970s practise around the ornamental fountain at the Welsh Folk Museum has to be seen to be believed. Superstition is irrational fear of the unknown and misdirected reverence. In this sense it is closely allied to religion of which it may indeed be a debased form. This is illustrated by the custom of an old man in north Montgomeryshire who, within living memory, used to place ashes on his head on Ash Wednesday and walked barefoot on that day the stony road to the top of a neighbouring hill. He gave as a reason for his action, 'my people have always done this and I would have no luck if I were to change the custom.' The Catholic custom of sprinkling ashes on a penitent's head on the first day of Lent had remained here throughout centuries of Protestantism and Dissent as a superstition maintained to bring luck. In the same way, the penitent's *peccavi* in confessing his sins remains in at least one west-Montgomeryshire dialect as *bicafio* in the sense of bowing down or cringing.

The development of religious or ecclesiastical organizations throughout the centuries throws much light on the continuity and development of tradition in the social life of rural communities in particular: it is less apparent in urban communities. In the Middle Ages, Catholicism had a firm hold on Wales, particularly the heart of Wales, the Welsh uplands. Here the people were Calvinist by nature, with the countryman's belief in Fate. They were grateful for an organized religion and for security of belief with an external authority on which they could depend. The Protestant Reformation—the church of Henry VIII—made no difference to their life or their beliefs, except that it took from them kindly priest and sheltering monastery alike. The dissenting sects—Quakers, Independents, Baptists and Presbyterian—which developed in the seventeenth century provided an intellectual religion for the individual. Here was no general confessional or traditional creed, no social religious system. Instead, these sects depended on small cells of covenanting believers who despised symbols and idols and whose only priest was Jesus Christ himself. It was not a religion to take the place of the medieval church.

But in the eighteenth century came the Calvinistic Methodist movement. This stressed man's sinfulness and inherent worthlessness. Its great hymn-writer, William Williams of Pantycelyn, wrote of man, 'I am dust, from dust I came, the worm is my brother, the earth my mother.' Like their forefathers in Catholic times, these country Methodists had strong ideas about God, the great Day of Judgement and the horned black devil, of heaven as a place and (as in medieval theology) of Christ as ransom for man's sins. As Milton had seen, the 'new presbyter', was but 'old priest writ large'. Holy Writ took the place of the Pope of Rome; its infallibility was undoubted. The Catholic hierarchy was replaced by the intricate machinery of the new church 'body', known colloquially as *Yr Hen*

Gorff ('the old body') reminiscent in its ramifications of the authoritarian 'body' of the medieval church. One of the significant innovations of this movement was the *seiad brofiad*, a meeting in which members confessed their sins and shortcomings before their brethren—a transmutation of the Catholic confessional.

Even in the twentieth century, the church 'body' was able to proscribe certain books in the manner of the Catholic *Index librorum prohibitorum*; and within the author's memory the high court of the denomination was still known to act as an Inquisition to throw out heretics. It was not the Puritans of the seventeenth century but this popular Methodist 'Reformation' of the following century which banned the harp and its folk tunes, the popular dancing and the Sunday games. At the same time it frowned severely on plays and novels alike. By the nineteenth century, a further transmutation had occurred: the folk tunes had become hymn tunes and added considerably to the glory of Welsh congregational singing. In so far as the older Nonconformity had espoused the methods and theology of the new movement, Wales became more thoroughly and universally a 'religious' country than it had been since the Middle Ages. Even the priestly chanting of the medieval church had become the *hwyl* of the reforming preachers. In one instance indeed, one of the leaders of the movement even established a monastic centre in Brecknockshire where attention was devoted not only to spiritual matters but to the development of agriculture. But it is important to realize that all this was more of a transmutation of the old traditional religion than the upthrust of a new one. To adapt the late W. R. Inge's phrase, popular ideas had revolved three hundred and fifty-nine degrees.

The older Independents laid little stress on creeds or even sacraments. To them a covenanting cell of believers was all important. The older Presbyterian churches evolved naturally into Unitarian congregations, the most tolerant and truly catholic of all sects. But the new Methodists formulated a lengthy and strict creed, *y Gyffes Ffydd*, the Confession of Faith. The Independents and Baptists espoused much of the Methodist theology and indeed of aspects of its church government and while they tended to become 'methodistized' the Quakers in Wales were squeezed out of existence and the Unitarians confined mainly to a small area of west Wales known, significantly, as 'the black spot'. In recent years when the universal tendency is to eschew small units and idealize the large—even the small farm is curtly denounced as nonviable—the need for denominational union is stressed in all directions while the ecumenical discussions of still more recent date call for a modern universal church to replace the medieval one. *Plus ça change, plus c'est la même-chose.*

Chapter 6

Music and Dance

The terms 'folk music' and 'folk dance' have a certain ambiguity which has caused much wrong thinking on this subject. The late Sir John Squire, for instance, held that 'folk-song springs from a life composed of a few simple elements . . .;—transport, the decay of agriculture and rural community life, education, modern amusements, mechanical music, and other factors, have destroyed the conditions which generated and preserved folk-song.'[1] My old friend, the late Iolo A. Williams, in the same volume,[2] states categorically: 'Folk, therefore, has here a restricted meaning; it means the English peasantry.' But he includes in 'peasantry'—itself a highly ambiguous term—not only 'agricultural labourers, cowmen, shepherds, woodmen, road-menders and other such rural wage-earners' but also 'small farmers and other country tradesmen' as well as 'the sailor-before-the-mast' and the street hawker. He qualifies his statement still further by arguing that 'the special connection of folk-song . . . with the peasantry is more often a matter of transmission than of origin'. Viewed from this standpoint, folk music is held to belong to a single stratum of rural society only (although the reference to the street 'hawker' tends dangerously to wreck the argument).

This attempt, widespread amongst many writers to this day, to isolate folk song and music to one class and that within a rural community is totally unacceptable. A. H. Fox Strangways admirably summarized the standpoint of the student of folk life when he wrote[3]

[1] Iolo A. Williams: *English Folk-Song and Dance*, London, 1935, page x.

[2] ibid., p. 1.

[3] *The Observer*, 19 June 1938.

'"Folk" means "all human beings". You are a member of the folk, so am I. "The folk" never meant "yokels", these . . . were the "lewde men" as opposed to "lettred men". There is ample evidence that what was sung and danced and acted in Langland's day was the same for all, and that in these occupations, castle and cottage met on equal footing: and though dame of high degree made one thing of them and serving-maid quite another, yet both shared one fancy and moved to one rhythm, as their modern counterparts may. What has happened is that song and dance that all knew and practised have survived chiefly among the unlettered who think little of mushroom growths; as have also the customs and courtesies and plain homely virtues of which they are the expression.'

It is no exaggeration to say, therefore, that folk song continues to be created amongst Glasgow bus-drivers as well as in the country-side, in school and university as well as in the stable-loft.

Here, another myth must be disposed of, namely that folk song, in some mysterious way, was always a corporate production, conceived and given birth to by a community of 'the folk'. This is arrant nonsense. Individuals wrote the original songs which became folk songs and individuals composed the original tunes which later became associated with them. Their names were generally unimportant and in many instances have long been unknown: the verses and the tunes have thereby earned the title of 'traditional' and have become 'folk song'.[1] Iolo A. Williams (ibid., p. 4) has even argued that 'it is because the English peasant was unable to read, because his was the only mind dependent upon sung words and airs for its knowledge of vocal music, that he became the sole vehicle for the transmission of these songs.' If he had only thought of his Welsh ancestor, Iolo Morganwg, himself the 'author' of many verses which became folk songs, he would have known that this old eighteenth-century stonemason and the 'peasantry' to which he belonged were well-able to read. The literate Welsh community of

[1] In the early 1930s I was asked by the late Sir Walford Davies to write a second verse to add to the one traditional verse of '*Cân y Gwŷdd*' (The Song of the Loom). This I did. When the University of Wales song book in which '*Cân y Gwŷdd*' was printed, appeared, I was amused to discover that the second (as well as the first) verse was described as 'traditional'!

the past two hundred years produced a wealth of folk song. 'A nameless author and a succession of nameless singers' wrote Cecil Sharp, 'who criticize by the way they perform the song, correspond to the composer's successive drafts, and the final result may be very different from the original.'[1]

How therefore does one define folk song and folk music? It is fundamentally *unlearned* artistry. To quote Iolo A. Williams again (this time with full approval!), 'each set of words, each air, no doubt originated in the mind of a single man or woman, but, by constant handing on from one singer to another, the personality of an individual author or composer has been eliminated and that of a nation . . . substituted.' I have used the term 'artistry' intentionally. 'Dr. Vaughan Williams', wrote Fox Strangways (op. cit.), 'does not say that a nameless, dateless folk-songster is as great a musician as Mozart: he says that *the musical impulse and ability* behind the "Wraggle-Taggles" are *the same in quality* as those behind the G minor quintet.' A traditional bowl produced by a Welsh turner cannot be compared with an Epstein bronze but the emotive impulse behind both is the same in essence.

Folk music, then, is music originating in the mind of a single person which in the course of time has taken on the personality of a community or a region or a nation.[2] Here one has to tread carefully, for it would be wrong to suggest that there can be *national* music or *national* painting. A perceptive literary critic[3] has declared that 'what makes an Englishman an Englishman, a Frenchman a Frenchman, a Russian a Russian, is first to speak the speech as his native tongue—that is all the nationality which a Government, not bent on national suicide, *dares* to take cognizance of—and, second, to have a national culture, a tradition, of which in his heart he is proud . . . You cannot be nationally proud of music, any more

[1] Maud Karpeles: *Cecil Sharp: his life and work*, London, 1967, p. 64.

[2] The definition of folk music adopted by the International Folk Music Council is 'music that has been submitted to the process of oral transmission. It is the product of evolution and is dependent on the circumstances of continuity, variation and selection.' (*International Folk Music Journal*, VII, 1955, p. 6.)

[3] J. Middleton Murry: 'Meditation on Heine', in *The Wanderer* (private subscription), 1934, p. 47.

than you can be nationally proud of painting. The art of words alone—poetry alone—is the appointed utterance of a national culture.' The late T. S. Eliot made a similar affirmation: 'No art is more stubbornly national than poetry'.[1] Folk music certainly has local characteristics and communicates something to the composer's compatriots which a foreigner will miss, but as Eliot holds,[2] 'at least within the circle of European culture, a good critic can form a sound opinion of the merit of foreign works of art: there are at least common laws of construction, common standards of technical mastery. And of all the forms of art for which language is used—the theatre, the novel, the prose work of every kind—poetry is the most indissoluble from its language. With poetry alone, we can never feel *quite* certain of our judgement, without the support of critics who belong to the same country and the same language.' Folk music is not national in this sense: it is national only when combined intimately with words. Emotion and feeling can only be fully expressed in folk music when the words of the vernacular language 'which a particular people has fashioned for itself through many generations and which in its turn has gone to fashion the mode of feeling of its people' are woven inextricably into it.

For example, many Welsh folk melodies became hymn-tunes during the past two centuries: they have also become international. But these airs sung to the words of a foreign language arouse in a Welshman only a shadow of the emotion and feeling which are engendered when the words traditionally linked with them are sung. Folk music cannot be considered in a national sense except in association with language.

This association between music and words developed in Wales a tradition peculiarly unique and one which it would be wrong to consider in the common connotation of 'folk music'. The courts of the Welsh princes had their official poets and harpists. Indeed when their status was regularized from time to time in the *eisteddfodau* held intermittently down to the sixteenth century, the badges of office included a small silver chair for the poet, a silver tongue for the

[1] T. S. Eliot: 'The Social Function of Poetry', in *The Adelphi*, 21, 1945, pp. 152–61.

[2] ibid.

singer and a silver harp for the harpist. These were small, to be worn over the left shoulder. The silver harp presented at the Caerwys (Flintshire) eisteddfod in 1567 is still extant (Plate 41). When the eisteddfod ceased to be a session for commissioning poets, singers and harpists and developed in the nineteenth century into a national folk festival, the small badge-chair 'grew' into a full-sized oak chair and has so remained to this day. In the same way (as we have seen, p. 67), the *gorsedd* stones 'grew' from Iolo Morganwg's pebbles into massive monoliths.

The Court poet composed eulogies, elegies and poems to his master's friends and acquaintances, asking for apparel, cattle, or implements and the like which his lord required. These poems—representing a *learned* artistry of a high order—praising the live or the dead (as the case might be) and describing a gown or an ox or an axe or even roofing tiles or a plough, are social documents of the highest value, and for the student of folk life, sources of much information. In addition, too, were the nature and love poems which bejewelled Welsh literature in the fourteenth century and later.

All the poems were written in the traditional 'strict metres' of which there were twenty-four kinds, the most popular, from the fourteenth century onwards, being the *cywydd deuair hirion* consisting of a series of rhymed couplets, each line being of seven syllables, the rhyme in the one line being accented and in the other unaccented. Each line is based on *cynghanedd*, i.e. 'harmony' in the sense that it is intricately and delicately shaped according to strict rules in the use of consonants and vowels. There are several forms of *cynghanedd* of which the easiest to illustrate, perhaps, is that in which the line consists of two parts, the consonants in the first part being answered in the second, e.g.

*F*y *n*ei*gr* aeth / o *f*ew*n* y *gr*o
A*r* er*ch*wy*nn*au / '*r* ar*ch* ho*nn*o

To a non-Welshman, this complexity may appear restrictive but many are the poets whom the discipline of *cynghanedd* has guided to ineffable beauty of expression. The 'strict' metre tradition has persisted to this day and has even entered, in recent times, somewhat paradoxically, into Welsh *vers libre*!

These poems were sung in the Courts: Miss Enid Roberts, of University College, Bangor, in a recent important paper,[1] has shown how the disciplines of poet and harpist were closely linked and how in musical training also there were twenty-four measures. In the second half of the sixteenth century, writes Miss Roberts, a subtle change came over the eulogies and elegies of the poets: they became less a pleasure to the ear than an appeal to the mind, things to be read rather than to be listened to. She suggests that it was at that time that the traditional *cywydd* of eulogy or elegy and the traditional harp and *crwth* music parted company. By that time Welshmen had become well-established in the Welsh Tudor Court and in London. They included musicians like Siôn Gwynedd (John Gwynneth, mid-sixteenth century), Richard Edwards (d. 1566) and later John Jenkins (1592–1678) and Robert Jones (late 16th–early 17th century). It was from that time onwards that one notices tunes such as *Grisial Ground, Leave Land, Heavy Heart, Crimson Velvet, Prettie Pussie, Hartes ease, Sweet Barbara* appearing as melodies for Welsh poems. 'There is today, so far as is known,'[2] (writes Dr. Thomas Parry) 'no written evidence that the poetry or music of England had any influence on Wales before the last half of the sixteenth century', but he hastens to add that this did 'not prove that such influence did not exist'. But it is fair to assume that the influence first became substantial in Tudor times.

The tradition before that period was, as we have seen, of a close link between the twenty-four metres of poetry and of the twenty-four measures of music. This, however, is a field into which the present writer has no competence to enter. We know, however, that a twelfth-century version of the Welsh Laws contains the following statement:

'When the King shall be pleased to hear songs in the hall, the *pencerdd* is to sing the first and the second song, namely one of God and the other of kings, and this in the upper part of the hall . . ., afterwards the *bardd teulu* shall sing the third song in the lower part

[1] Enid Roberts: 'Marwnadau Telynorion', in the *Transactions of the Denbighshire Historical Society*, 15, 1966, pp. 80–117.

[2] Thomas Parry: *A history of Welsh Literature*, translated by Sir H. Idris Bell, Oxford, 1955, p. 169.

of the hall . . . When the Queen shall desire to hear songs in her chamber, the *bardd teulu* is to sing to her three songs of finished art . . .'[1]

The *pencerdd* was the chief of song, and the *bardd teulu* the household poet, one of the officers of the court. 'Of the actual music of these vanished centuries', states Crossley-Holland,[2] 'nothing remains . . . But by a singular miracle of preservation, a manuscript of harp music which can lead us towards the music of those times yet survives.' It is of seventeenth-century date but contains music which Crossley-Holland and others believe 'may with great probability be dated to the fourteenth and fifteenth centuries'. Much of it consists of 'evidently musical accompaniments, either to songs whose words are now lost, or to the improvisations [?] of poets who, on occasion, like Dafydd ap Gwilym in the fourteenth century, wrote and sang both poems and music . . . Other pieces are conceived for harp alone.' Crossley-Holland takes the view that here are unmistakable examples 'of a systematic medieval chordal art' significant 'for the whole of musical history in the western world'.

Penillion singing is an ancient but still existing form of singing in Wales, indeed according to the late Dr. Percy Scholes,[3] 'known only in Wales . . . it consists in singing . . . poems' which may rhyme internally as well as line by line 'to an original counterpoint woven around some well-known melody played in a harmonized version by a harper'. The sung counterpoint is not in the same metre as the harper's melody and an expert singer is even able 'to extemporize a triple-time counterpoint to a duple-time melody and vice versa'. The origin of this singing which has attained much popularity in recent times is still obscure and may well be part of a medieval—if not earlier—tradition. Undoubtedly it reaches its perfection in the singing of poems in the traditional 'strict' metres; in the opinion of many, the recent tendency to set 'free' verse in this medium is by comparison unsuccessful.

[1] Sir H. Idris Bell: *The Nature of Poetry as conceived by the Welsh Bards*. The Taylorian Lecture, 1955, Oxford, p. 7.

[2] Peter Crossley-Holland: *Music in Wales*, London, 1948, p. 12.

[3] Percy A. Scholes: *The Oxford Companion to Music*, Oxford, 1938, p. 1009.

The three traditional instruments of Welsh music are the harp, the *crwth* and the pipes. Bagpipes were known in Wales and there are literary allusions to them. Giraldus Cambrensis (d. 1223) wrote that the Welsh 'make use of three instruments, the harp, *the pipes*, and the crwth' (though the plural 'pipes' does not refer to the bagpipe for which the old form was in the singular until more pipes were added).[1] But Iolo Goch (fourteenth century) refers to *chwibenigl a chod*, 'pipe and bag', while Lewis Glyn Cothi (fifteenth century) in a poem to the Englishmen of Flint likens the noise of the heron-voiced bagpipe to the howling of a 'sad, hoarse bitch imprisoned in a chest'. A fifteenth-century carving in the chancel roof of Llaneilian church, Anglesey[2] (Plate 42), depicts a bagpipe and there are illustrations in Hafod MS. 24 (1605–10). Giraldus's 'pipes' referred not only to the bagpipes but to the *pibgorn* and associated hornpipes which remained in use until the nineteenth century.

The *crwth* according to all known examples is a six-stringed instrument, oblong, with a flat back, sides and sound-board. It has a rectangular opening at the upper end divided into two by the finger-board. It has six strings, four stretched over the finger-board and two outside it. It is played with a bow. There are two circular holes in the sound-board and one of the feet of the bridge passed through one of these holes in the belly and rested on the back thus serving as a sound-post. The bridge was practically flat-topped, 'a circumstance from which it is to be inferred that two or three strings are to be sounded at the same time so as to afford a succession of concords. The bridge is not placed at right angles with the sides of the Crwth but in an oblique direction'.[3] The late Arnold Dolmetsch, commenting on this stated that with a flat bridge 'the obliquity would facilitate the bowing. But then only the Treble string could be fingered for different notes, the other strings serving as drones.'[4] In his reconstruction of a *crwth*, Dolmetsch ignored both the flat top and the 'obliquity'!

[1] F. W. Galpin: *Old English Instruments of Music*, 3rd Ed., London, 1932, p. 68.

[2] *Inventory of Ancient Monuments in Anglesey*, London, 1937, Plate 80.

[3] Edward Jones: *Musical and Poetical Relicks of the Welsh Bards*, London, 1794, p. 115.

[4] In a letter dated 28.2.1935.

Examples of the *crwth* have survived from the eighteenth century (Plate 43) and are to be found in the Welsh Folk Museum, the National Library of Wales and the Corporation Museum, Warrington. A *crwth* in the Museum of Fine Arts, Boston, U.S.A., was made about 1896 by a native of Merioneth, Owen Tudur (1813–1909), who had played it. There are other examples in the Gesellschaft der Musikfreunde, Vienna, and in the Conservatoire Royal de Musique, Brussels. The Vienna example has a small metal plate engraved with a bust of a soldier of the seventeenth century and though described as a Welsh *crwth*, its history is unknown. The Brussels example may be a rough copy of an eighteenth-century instrument. Here it is well to record that the late Canon Galpin informed me that copies of the eighteenth-century *crwth* which is now in the Welsh Folk Museum (and which had been shown in the London Exhibition, 1872) were made in the late nineteenth century by Chanot of Wardour Street for the Victoria and Albert Museum and for several continental museums. At least one of these reproductions, that in the Victoria and Albert Museum, was for many years mistaken for the original.[1]

In 1890, the late Henry Balfour published an account of the 'British hornpipe'.[2] This was of course the *pibgorn* of Wales, and the *stockhorn* of Scotland. More or less similar instruments are to be found in the Basque country, in the Greek archipelago and in Asian countries as far afield as China. The instrument consists of a wooden pipe with six finger-holes and a thumb-hole. It has a bell-mouth of a part of a cow's horn, with a serrated edge, and a mouth-piece also of horn. In the mouth-piece is placed a beating reed on the clarinet principle, formed by slitting the small reed-piece from above downwards, leaving the lower end of the vibrating tongue thus formed, fixed. The length of these instruments varies from about

[1] For example Otto Andersson: *The Bowed Harp*, London, 1930, p. 218: '. . . the Welsh National Museum . . . only possesses a copy of the South Kensington instrument.' The reverse is the truth, but in fairness to the author it should be stated that while the London instrument is a copy, the original reached the National Museum of Wales after 1930.

[2] Henry Balfour: 'The Old British "Pibcorn" or "Hornpipe" and its affinities', in *Journal of the Anthropological Institute*, XX, 1890, pp. 142–54.

sixteen to twenty inches. Two examples of the Welsh *pibgorn* are in the Welsh Folk Museum; one (the property of the Society of Antiquaries of London) comes from Anglesey and was described in the 1775 volume of *Archaeologia*. The late Canon Galpin informed me that the reed fitted in it was made by him. The other (Plate 44) (the property of Col. J. C. Wynne-Finch) is also believed to have come originally from Anglesey. The oldest illustration of such an instrument in England is in a fifteenth-century window in St. Mary's Church, Warwick. Canon Galpin told me that his friends in Dolgellau remembered the *pibgorn* well in the Berwyn hills, while another writer (David Griffith, *Clwydfardd*, 1800–84) stated in 1892 that 'about a century ago' the *pibgorn* was commonly heard in south Wales, the servant-men carrying them with them when driving cattle to the fairs. Balfour's statement that the world distribution of this instrument 'agrees with that of the megalithic monuments' should not be taken seriously.

The harp has been linked consistently with the music of the Keltic nations: it is undoubtedly an instrument which has been greatly favoured by them throughout the centuries. For instance, in the Welsh Laws the harp was one of the three indispensables of the freeman. In *The Book of Taliesin* (*c.* 1275), the harpist, *crythor*, and the piper are all mentioned. Galpin[1] maintained dogmatically that it was 'the Angle, the Saxon and the North men who used the harp' and that it was taken over by the Keltic peoples after the tenth century. This is difficult to believe when it is known that the Welsh Laws in which the harp figures prominently were codified in the tenth century. O'Curry,[2] too, was 'certain' that the Irish never borrowed the instrument which is the first musical instrument referred to in early Irish writings. Hortense Panum[3] holds that Galpin was incorrect in attributing the framed harp to the Northern peoples and that the harp proper was 'first found in the British Isles'. It is however dangerous to dogmatize in this way: Galpin could

[1] op. cit., p. 10.

[2] E. O'Curry: *On the Manners and Customs of the Ancient Irish*, London, 1873, p. 213.

[3] Hortense Panum: *The Stringed Instruments of the Middle Ages*. London, 1941, pp. 102 ff.

quote in favour of this theory, Venantius Fortunatus who was bishop of Poitiers between A.D. 599 and 609 who averred that

. . . plaudat tibi barbarus harpa . . . crotta Britanna canat.

As Jarman[1] has pointed out, *harpa* is a Teutonic form which has given *harfe* in German and 'harp' in English. *Crotta*, on the other hand, is the *crot* (later *cruit*) or harp of the Irish, and the *crwth* of the Welsh. It has been suggested by several writers (Galpin, Andersson and others) that the Irish *cruit* like the Welsh *crwth* was a bowed instrument similar in type to a widespread European form, in short a bowed 'harp' whose name was transferred later to the framed harp until the name *clarséach* supplanted it.

In the Middle Ages, the harps of Ireland, Scotland and Wales were of *clarséach* type. Some had horsehair strings (Welsh *telyn rawn*), some wire, others had gut (W. *coludd*), and others leather (*lledr*), while in some cases the frame was leather-covered:

For my harpe is made of a mares skyn
The stringes be of horse heare,
it maketh a good din.[2]

as a sixteenth-century rhymester averred. The *clarséach*, a small harp, was revived in both Scotland and Wales in the present century.

The harp linked with Wales, however, and often referred to—quite erroneously—as the 'traditional' Welsh harp is the triple-strung harp; 'the two outer ranks are identically tuned to a diatonic scale, the centre rank is tuned to the intervening chromatic notes, plus two in each octave which are identical with two in the outer ranks.'[3] This form of harp was devised in Italy in the late years of the sixteenth or the early years of the seventeenth century. 'It was one of many early baroque inventions or adaptations in the field of large-range chromatic instruments.'[4] Miss Rimmer adds that the

[1] A. O. H. Jarman: 'Telyn a Chrwth', in *Llên Cymru*, VI, 1960–1, p. 171.

[2] Andrew Borde: *The Fyrst Boke of the Introduction of Knowledge* (1547 *or* 8), reprinted in Early English Texts Society, Extra Series, X, edit. F. J. Furnivall, 1870, pp. 125–6.

[3] Joan Rimmer: 'The morphology of the triple harp', in *The Galpin Society Journal*, XVIII, pp. 90–103.

[4] ibid., p. 90.

41. Silver harp, Caerwys (Flintshire) Eisteddfod 1567

42. Bagpipe player, carving in the chancel roof of Llaneilian church, Anglesey. 15th century

43. *Crwth*, dated 1742, from Caernarvonshire (in the Welsh Folk Museum)

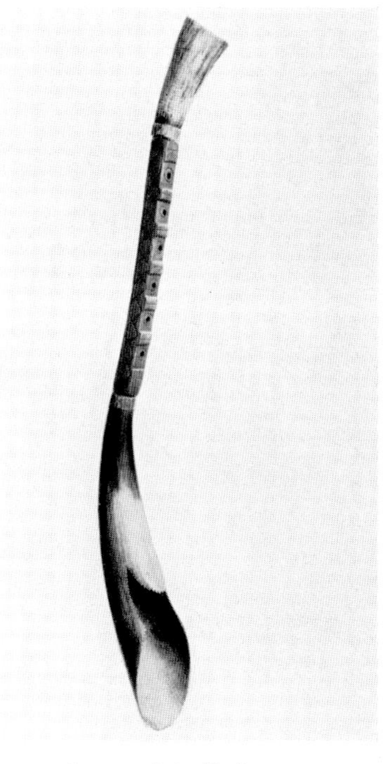

44. *Pibgorn*, originally from Anglesey. 18th century (in the Welsh Folk Museum)

45. *Mari Lwyd*, from Pen-tyrch, Glamorgan (in the Welsh Folk Museum)

46. *Láir Bhán*, as found in Ireland and the Isle of Man. *Photo: National Museum of Ireland*

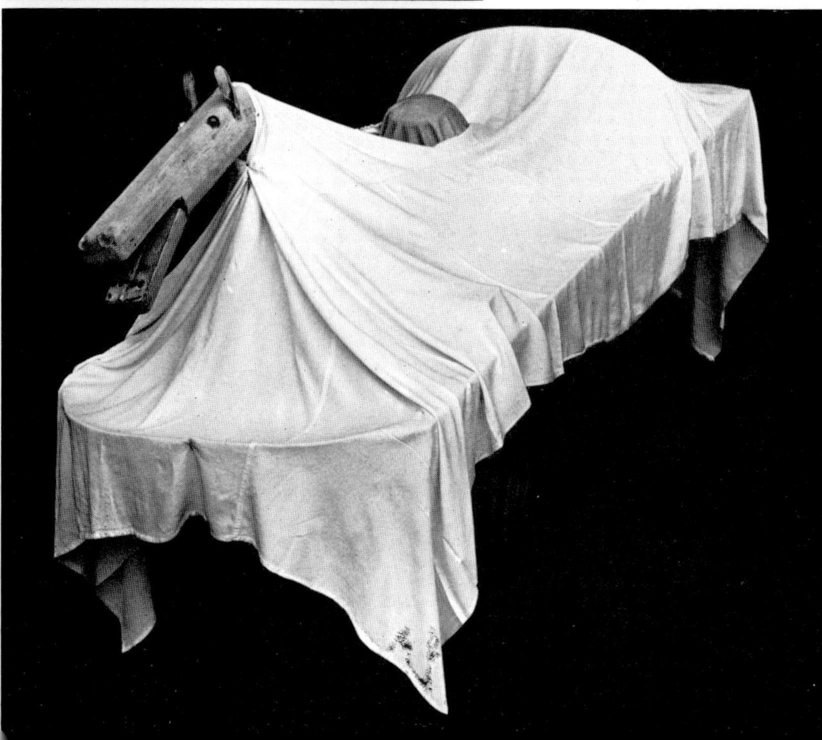

47. Wren house, from Pembrokeshire (in the Welsh Folk Museum)

48. The Denbigh cockpit (in the Welsh Folk Museum)

49. Wassail bowl, 1834, of Ewenni (Glamorgan) ware (in the Welsh Folk Museum)

triple harp, 'with little traceable history in its country of origin, has survived to the present day, though tenuously, in Wales, in musical and social contexts as far removed from its aristocratic baroque origins as could be imagined.' She points out that in England at the Restoration was one Charles Evans, the 'harper for the Italian harp'. One wonders whether, with such a name, he was Welsh. Miss Rimmer adds that 'from the end of the seventeenth century onwards, the instrument's history belongs almost exclusively to Wales'. The Welsh Folk Museum possesses an example which Miss Rimmer dates as late seventeenth or early eighteenth century. This must be the earliest evidence extant of the triple harp in Wales. Mrs. Margaret Davies of Coetgae-du, Trawsfynydd, writing to Dafydd Jones of Trefriw on the 26th June, 1758, states:

'ac wele yn awr Delynau Tri phâr Danau gan bob math agos'[1]
[and now we see triple-strung harps in the possession of almost all sorts.]

The triple harp had become generally popular in that area by the 1750s. If it is a 'traditional' Welsh harp, the tradition is only two hundred years old. Such harps were produced in the second half of the eighteenth century by the harp-maker, John Richards of Llanrwst (1711–89), who also worked for many years in south Wales and in the nineteenth century by another harp-maker, Bassett Jones of Cardiff, who in 1843, to the order of Lady Llanover, produced a florid rococo gilt harp (now in the Welsh Folk Museum) for presentation to, and inscribed, *Albert Prince of Wales* (subsequently King Edward VII). But by the end of the first quarter of the nineteenth century the standard European pedal harp was beginning to be used in Wales and throughout the nineteenth century it gradually supplanted the triple-strung variety. At the present time one notable player remains who received early training on the triple harp: she is Mrs. Nansi Richards Jones. She has trained several others; some other harpists, such as the distinguished harpist, Dr. Osian Ellis, are also proficient triple-harp players.

[1] G. J. Williams (ed.): *Llythyrau at Ddafydd Jones o Drefriw.* National Library of Wales *Journal* Supplement, Aberystwyth, 1943, p. 19.

Miss Rimmer (op. cit.) in discussing baroque performance practice, concludes that though

'the triple harp cannot be counted a mainstream baroque instrument, nevertheless it is the only baroque art instrument on which there has been a continuous tradition of performance. The steel-fingered techniques learnt by Nansi Richards Jones in childhood from rural players and gypsies, the striking of the harp, the playing close to the belly for clarity and sonority, were part of a non-written tradition preserved in conservative social circumstances. While it would be imprudent to assume that this playing represents an unchanged baroque style, it is reasonable to think that its characteristic features—in many cases the opposite of pedal harp techniques include at least some which were part of seventeenth-century practice. Mrs. Richards Jones's performance, both disciplined and passionate, embodies a very different concept of musical sound and style from that generally associated with performance of baroque music today.'

* * *

Dancing is an activity as old as man himself for it is obvious from archaeological and pictorial evidence, from the literature of successive ages and from a study of primitive peoples throughout the world that various dance rituals have been performed at all times. (The study of these rituals does not here concern us: the subject is vast and complicated and has been discussed throughout the ages by many specialists.)[1]

Great Britain and Ireland were no exception. But it is true to say that a high degree of industrialization tended to kill off or at least to submerge many of the dances whose ritual was connected with pastoral and agricultural pursuits. It is also true that while many dance rituals had a religious significance, the growth of literacy with a detailed knowledge of the Bible (as, for example in eighteenth and nineteenth-century Wales) and of the Christian religion as a personal faith strengthened in the meetings of organized churches

[1] Amongst the most recent are Walter Sorell: *The Dance through the Ages*, London, 1967, and Joan Lawson: *European Folk Dance*, London, 1967.

tended to kill the dance which was considered to be a part of the pagan past. Organized Nonconformist denominations, strongly Calvinist in theology with a strong emphasis on the need for 'saving' the individual soul placed a taboo on the 'pagan foolishness' of dancing, a taboo which has not yet completely disappeared from several rural districts in England, Scotland and Wales. It is no accident that the modern revival of folk dancing coincides with the break-up of institutional religion in this island.

At the same time, English critics, in particular, should be chary of making sweeping generalizations in this context concerning their neighbours: for the myth of the 'Keltic twilight' is still much in evidence. Joan Lawson,[1] writing of the Welsh as 'a nation of singers', states categorically that 'yet few Welsh tunes have a dancing rhythm, for they are predominantly solemn and sad'. This is completely untrue as even a cursory glance at the many collections of Welsh folk tunes will prove. Nor should one forget the many references in Welsh literature (and by English travellers in Wales) to communal dancing of many kinds. Unfortunately the vast majority of English students of folk dance pass categorical judgements on folk dancing in Ireland, Scotland and Wales without first equipping themselves with even an elementary knowledge of the Gaelic, Irish and Welsh languages in each of which so much evidence survives.

Amongst the dances associated with animals, one of the most interesting and most widespread is that commonly known as the Hobby Horse. Lawson (op. cit.) has suggested that 'these strange creatures are possibly the last remnants of the horse-worshipping rites belonging to the nomadic tribes of Europe and Asia who domesticated this animal. The horse is an extremely useful beast, providing a means of transport as well as food and drink, and because it was a vital element in the struggle for survival, rituals evolved which man hoped would ensure its continued fertility. The leader would dress up in the horse's skin, make a head-dress of his skull, imitate his movements and indulge in activities which have now degenerated into those antics of the Padstow Hobby-Horse, where he whisks a girl under his skirt, or noses round the girls' legs.'

[1] op. cit. *supra*, p. 171.

The details of this theory should be accepted with reserve for to prove them is now impossible. We are told that horse dances occur in the Basque country, Hungary, Poland and Russia. They are much more widespread reaching as far as from Java to Ireland. The Hobby-Horses of such places as Minehead and Padstow, the *Mari Lwyd* (Grey Mare) of Wales (Plate 45) and *Láir Bhán* (White Mare) of Ireland[1] and the Isle of Man (Plate 46) are all variants of the same ritual dance, which in some instances has deteriorated to a money-making processional from house to house. A variant of a more unusual form used to be found in Pembrokeshire: it was called *Y March* (The Horse or the Stallion) or indeed *Y Gynfas-farch* (The Canvas Horse). A canvas sheet used for carrying corn-chaff or the *brethyn rhawn* (horse-hair sheet) used over the kiln for drying corn was sewn at one of the corners for about a yard to form a front and a head. The eyes were represented by large buttons and two brown harvest gloves tacked on for ears. The head was tightly stuffed with straw. The player stood underneath the canvas and a pitchfork stuck into the straw enabled him to turn the head about in every direction. This prowling monster could peep into rooms or push his head through an upstairs window, even causing sudden death through fright on some occasions. In England and in Wales, these performances were possibly to some degree influenced by the mumming tradition in England. Miss Violet Alford,[2] in a discussion of the 'Plough play' on the first Monday after 6th January, refers to 'most interesting Hobby horses made of farm riddles, horse and man covered with a "housing" right over the man's head' at Tollerton, Notts.

These horse customs, now looked upon as folklore, were undoubtedly all related to ritual dances. Some, such as the Welsh *Mari Lwyd*, involved poetical dialogues between the 'horse' party and the folk inside the houses, similar to the 'poetical contests' in Portugal, often between a man and a woman in which verse follows verse until one of the two competitors is discomfited.[3] Some are associated with the beginning of spring and wassailing elements are

[1] Iorwerth C. Peate: 'Mari Lwyd–Láir Bhán', in *Folk Life*, I, 1963, pp. 95–6.
[2] Violet Alford: *Sword Dance and Drama*, London, 1962, p. 57.
[3] Rodney Gallop: *Portugal; a book of folk-ways*, Cambridge, 1936, p. 221.

introduced (e.g. *Mari Lwyd*), some with such festivals as Plough Monday etc. At some stage in their history, they were taken into the Christian church and partly sublimated to its purpose. For example, the *Mari Lwyd* was given a veneer of Catholic songs to Mary, so that the name itself was later misinterpreted as 'Holy Mary'. Even in the nineteenth century, we come across such incongruous folk-song references as '*Mari a Joseff, y gath a'r ci*' (Mary and Joseph, the cat and the dog). In this respect, it has been suggested to me[1] that even the words of some Welsh hymns are adaptations of folk verse in the way that their tunes are of folk music.

Another ritual dance which later deteriorated into a noisy processional can be found in the numerous examples of 'hunting the wren' which, practised from St. Stephen's Day—Boxing Day—to the 6th January (Twelfth Day) in Ireland, the Isle of Man, and Wales, is also found further afield in Europe. This processional gave rise in Wales to a wealth of folk song, the variants of the verses being very numerous, representing several Welsh counties from Denbighshire to Pembrokeshire. In this last mentioned county it survived at least well into the second half of the nineteenth century. Many of the melodies and songs have been recorded and published in the first volume of the *Journal* of the Welsh Folk-Song Society. In Wales, the wren Procession took place on Twelfth Night, the wren being carried in a 'house' (Plate 47) on a bier by two or three men, the house and bier bedecked with ribbons. The custom is described in the seventeenth century by Edward Lhuyd.[2]

Such rituals as those mentioned above must be considered seriously in any discussion of the folk dance although unfortunately the detailed movements of the dances have long been lost, as they deteriorated along the years into a procession. Both the horse and the wren rituals were principally associated with the period from All Hallows' Eve to Twelfth Night. Others, of a different nature belonged to the month of May—the maypole rituals were well-known in Wales as in England—and to high mid-summer, St.

[1] By my colleague, Mr. R. Gwyndaf Jones.

[2] See his 'Parochialia', in *Arch. Camb.*, 1910, p. 82: and also Iorwerth C. Peate: 'The Wren in Welsh Folklore', in *Man*, 1936, No. 1.

John's Eve. The *Cadi Ha'* is an obvious example. *Y fedwen haf* ('the summer birch') was erected in many Glamorgan villages and gaily decorated with flowers and ribbons for the feast of St. John.[1] The dancers even had a wooden building called *pebyll* ('pavilion') where they kept their dresses and often met to dance and sing. (G. J. Williams mentions that the well-known air *Triban Morgannwg* is a dance tune.) But the death-knell of such dancing was tolled when Charles Wesley, on his preaching tours, came to Wales in 1741, writing in his *Journal* that he preached in one village on the text of 'revellings, banquetings, and abominable idolatries'. He adds: 'An old dancer of three score fell down under the stroke of the hammer. She could never be convinced before that there was any harm in those innocent pleasures.' It was Wesley and his fellow-workers in the Methodist revivals of the eighteenth century, and not the earlier Puritans, who began the destruction of the traditional dances.

Research and diligent collecting, during the present century, in the four countries of these islands, have brought to the surface much information concerning song and dance. It may still be not too late to find that somewhere an obscure countryman or a village housewife may, even now, be able to provide much information to fill many gaps in our knowledge of an almost forgotten tradition.

[1] G. J. Williams: 'Glamorgan Customs in the eighteenth century', in *Gwerin*, I, 1956–7, p. 104.

Chapter 7

Play

We have seen that ritual has played a prominent part in the development of national cultures. As Lewis Mumford stresses:[1] 'At the beginning . . . ritual and language [see Chapter 6] were the chief means of maintaining order and establishing human identity.' Ritual was the groundwork for man's later higher development. Indeed A. M. Hocart has suggested that 'even the first great division of labour may have been established in ritual, with its fixed offices and functions, before it was carried over into technology.'[2] Undoubtedly, ritual was the groundwork for much of man's leisure activities—in the fields of cultural institutions and education, religion, and in sport and games. The concept of ritual as 'a detached series of collective acts' of a special quality to which the term 'sacred' is attached is well known and the creation of this 'realm of the sacred' can well be looked upon, as Mumford asserts, as 'one of the decisive steps in the transformation of man,' for it served as 'a connecting link between the seen and the unseen, the temporal and the eternal.'

Much of man's play originated in this sector of human experience, as we have seen in discussing aspects of the dance. In south-west Wales, in parts of which the old New Year's Day (Yr Hen Galan, 12th January) is still observed, and indeed in other parts of south Wales, variants of a ball game called *cnapan* were popular throughout the centuries and in some areas in Pembrokeshire, south Cardiganshire and west Carmarthenshire, the *cnapan* game took a ritualistic guise during the New Year festivities. The game in the

[1] Lewis Mumford: *The Myth of the Machine*, London, 1967, p. 78.
[2] ibid.

sixteenth century was described by George Owen (1552–1613), the historian of Pembrokeshire:[1]

'This game is called *cnapan* and not unfitly as shall be showed, the game is thought to be of great antiquity and is as followeth. The ancient Britons being naturally a warlike nation did no doubt for the exercise of their youth in time of peace and to avoid idleness devise games of activity where each man might show his natural prowess and agility, as some for strength of the body by wrestling, lifting of heavy burdens, others for the arm as in casting the bar, sledge, stone, or hurling the bawl or ball, others that excelled in swiftness of foot, to win the praise therein by running, and surely for the exercise of the parts aforesaid this *cnapan* was prudently invented, had the same continued without abuse thereof. For in it, beside the exercise of the bodily strength, it is not without resemblance of warlike providence, as shall be hereafter declared, and first before I describe you the play, I will let you know that this *cnapan* happens and falls out to be by two means. The one is a settled or standing *cnapan* the date and place being known and yearly haunted and observed: of these *cnapan* days in Pembrokeshire there were wont to be five in number, the first at Bury sands between the parishes of Nevern and Newport upon Shrove Tuesday yearly; the second at Portheinon, on Easter Monday, between the parishes of Meline and Eglwyswrw; the third on Low Easterday at Pwll-du in Penbedw between the parishes Penrhydd and Penbedw; the fourth and fifth were wont to be at St. Meigans in Cemais between Cemais men of the one party, and Emlyn men, and the men of Cardiganshire with them of the other party, the first upon Ascension Day, the other upon Corpus Christi day, and these two last were the great and main places, far exceeding any of the former in multitude of people for at these places there have often times been esteemed two thousand foot beside horsemen . . .

'. . . About one or two of the clock afternoon begins the play, in this sort, after a cry made both parties draw together into some plain, all first stripped bare saving a light pair of breeches, bare-

[1] George Owen: *The Description of Pembrokeshire*. Edited by Henry Owen. Vols. 1–4, London, 1892, I, pp. 270 ff.

headed, bare-bodied, bare legs and feet . . . for if he leave but his shirt on his back in the fury of the game, it is most commonly torn to pieces and I have also seen some long-lock gallants, trimly trimmed at this game not by clipping but by pulling their hair and beards.

'The foot company thus meeting, there is a round ball prepared of a reasonable quantity so as a man may hold it in his hand and no more, this ball is of some massy wood as box, yew, crab or holly tree and should be boiled in tallow for to make it slippery and hard to hold. This ball is called *cnapan* and is by one of the company hurled bolt upright into the air, and at the fall he that catches it hurls it towards the country he plays for, for goal or appointed place there is none neither needs any, for the play is not given over until the *cnapan* be so far carried that there is no hope to return it back that night, for the carrying of it a mile or two miles from the first place is no losing of the honour so it be still followed by the company and the play still maintained, it is often times seen the chase to follow two miles and more . . . It is a strange sight to see a thousand or fifteen hundred naked men to concur together in a cluster in following the *cnapan* as the same is hurled backward and forward' . . .[1]

Owen's account has been quoted here at length because of its descriptive value. It continues for several pages drawing attention to the value of the back players, the 'borderers', the 'good footmanship', the guile of the forward players who control the direction of the game, and the skill of 'hurling' in a tight situation so that 'it lighteth to some of his fellows'. The horsemen also take part, being allowed to use 'cudgells' in certain situations, against which the call was *heddwch, heddwch* ('peace, peace'), the same call, by a strange coincidence, as is today found in the chairing ceremony at an eisteddfod! It has been argued that despite the differences in the two games, the *cnapan* tradition may well have predisposed the Welsh towards their love of and skill in rugby football. Be that as it may, the tradition persisted: in the Llandysul area of south Cardiganshire until 1922. Here was held on the first day of the Julian calendar a mass football match in which the goals were eight miles

[1] The orthography has been modernized.

apart, at the churches of Llandysul and Llanwenog. The disorder and unruliness became so great that in 1922 'the whole business was transmuted into a Sunday School festival which still flourishes.'[1]

It is a far cry from the sixteenth-century hurling game to a twentieth-century singing festival but such a transmutation provides a good example of how folk ritual and tradition are sublimated and metamorphosed in the course of time.

A game well-known in England from Yorkshire and Lancashire through the Midlands and home counties as far west as Devonshire is that of bandy, a game very similar to hockey and played with sticks bent and round at one end and a small wooden ball. This was known in Wales as *bando*, a game known throughout the country in varying forms and still to be found in some areas. The earliest example of the Welsh term *bando* occurs in a dictionary by John Walters published in 1770–94. It was particularly popular in the Cynffig-Margam district of the Vale of Glamorgan where wide stretches of sandy beaches afforded ample room for play. The 'Margam Bando Boys', at the turn of the eighteenth–nineteenth centuries, were celebrated in song in both English and Welsh:

Due praises I'll bestow
And all the world shall know
That Margam valour shall keep its colour
While Kenfig's waters flow.

Our master, straight and tall,
Is foremost with the ball;
He is, we know it and must allow it,
The fastest man of all.

Let cricket players blame
And seek to slight our fame,
Their bat and wicket can never lick it,
This ancient manly game.

[1] *Manchester Guardian*, 12.1.1959.

Our fame shall always stand
Throughout Britannia's land;
What man can beat us? Who dare to meet us?
Upon old Kenfig's strand.

Further descriptions of this game can be found in G. J. Williams (op. cit.). Another ball game mentioned in a Welsh poem as early as the fifteenth century was tennis, *gware . . . tenis* ('playing tennis'). 'In my early days', wrote Mathew Owen of Anglesey who was born in 1769, 'we went of a Sunday morning to the cemetery before the service to tell tales and to boast of football, wrestling, slinging stones and the like; then to the service. In the afternoon we went to play the tennis ball on to the roof of the church.' Many indeed were the games which were played in the churchyard and even in the church porch. The Rev. Elias Owen refers[1] to 'card playing, dice throwing and other such like games' and quotes the register for 1698–1719 of Trelawnyd (or Newmarket) church, Flintshire, in which it is stipulated that the 'ministers and churchwardens . . . are to appoint each of them an old man, and where old men are wanting, then an old woman, and enter their names in the Church Book on the 29th day of December yearly and every year for ever, that they the said old men or old women . . . may draw Lots or throw Dice for such Quantity of Flanen [=flannel, Welsh *gwlanen*] as shall be bought with the yearly interest of . . . two pounds and ten shillings on the Feast of Epiphany yearly and every year for ever.' The dice were to be thrown 'in the church porch at such time of the day as the said minister shall openly appoint on Sunday next before.' Entries for 1712 and 1713 appear in the Register. As Owen comments, 'so minute are these directions that one cannot avoid coming to the conclusion that dice throwing was then a common practice.' Several other games too have a long history in these islands. Chess ('*gwyddbwyll*') is mentioned in the Mabinogion, and in the county of Glamorgan a 'fox-and-geese' game which is of considerable antiquity survived until at least the last century under the Welsh name '*stôl ganddo*' ('the fox's chair'). The old classical puzzle said to be of Chinese origin and called 'Chinese Rings' was

[1] In *Cymru Fu*, 2.11.1889, pp. 67–8.

popular in the mid-Wales countryside during my own childhood and I have collected examples, blacksmith made, from such then isolated rural areas as Trawsfynydd in Merioneth and Chwilog in Caernarvonshire. But even fifty years ago, one or two enterprising mail-order firms in London were exporting mass-produced 'tiring irons' (as the Chinese rings are sometimes called) into the Welsh countryside. The rural wood-turners and joiners also produced 'puzzles', often in boxwood, of a most intricate nature, which served to divert the local youth during many long winter hours. Newcomers, such as the lead miners of west Montgomeryshire and north Cardiganshire in the nineteenth century, often brought their own diversions from as far afield as Cornwall. In the tavern at Trefeurig in Cardiganshire a kind of roulette known as 'Billy Fair Play' was very popular amongst the miners. Other games such as cribbage and Pope Joan were popular in some parts.

Cockfighting has a long history in Europe and in the New World. It is said that the Romans introduced it into Britain and that it returned to popularity with the return of the Crusaders. Henry VIII was a keen follower of the 'game' and added a cockpit to Whitehall: after the fire of 1697, this became—by a strange irony—the Privy Council Room. Disapproved during Cromwell's Protectorate, cockfighting regained its popularity by the eighteenth century and there were throughout Wales several well-known cockpits. One, a well-known building with a thatched roof, in the town of Denbigh, has recently been re-erected in the Welsh Folk Museum (Plate 48). Many of the contests were held on Sunday afternoons: R. W. Jones[1] stated (1931) that a Llangadfan (Mont.) man then over eighty years of age remembered hearing the local sexton explain how his father used to announce in church 'There will be a cockfight at half past two, and our respected parson will place a quart of ale at the foot of Dafydd Ty'n Ffridd's cock.' In the course of time this barbarous game was made illegal but rumours are still heard occasionally of cockfights in localities whose names are kept secret.

Organized games—*hen chwaraeon y Cymry*, as Iolo Morganwg

[1] R. W. Jones: *Bywyd Cymdeithasol Cymru yn y Ddeunawfed Ganrif*, London, 1931, p. 112.

described them—were held in certain parts of Wales at definite periods of the year.[1] Summer games were held every Saturday throughout the summer and on until All Hallows' Day. Games were connected with the *bedwen haf* ('the summer birch'), which was often raised for the feast of St. John. G. J. Williams quotes a contemporary eighteenth-century description of an attempted theft of a 'summer birch' (which is called 'the May pole') by the villagers of St. Nicholas from its setting in St. Fagans village.

Life in the twentieth century has so revolutionized social custom that all these games have disappeared, except for the tenuous survival in one or two areas of the 'revels' related to the Christmas season. But much work on the literature of past centuries should result in a fair picture of the way in which our forebears played. This is one of the tasks of the student of folk life.

[1] G. J. Williams: op. cit., p. 101.

Chapter 8

Folk Lore

Several aspects of folk lore have been touched upon in previous chapters but the subject deserves a more extended attention, although several authoritative works (see Bibliography) have been published on it. To one who believes in the unity of the natural order to which man like all other animals belongs, no mystery can remain inexplicable for ever nor is it to be explained only by invoking the 'supernatural'. But throughout man's history, those phenomena which he could not then explain because of his lack of knowledge of the order of the natural world—e.g. thunder and lightning, rain and drought—were attributed to supernatural intervention. This lack of knowledge became the basis of folk lore. Naturally, much of this lore was related to the elemental areas of life, to the 'mystery' of birth and death and of the regular cycle of the seasons.The beliefs and customs relating to death provide one of the richest veins of folk lore as many works on the subject testify.

In some districts the belief that man is warned of his coming death, and that in no uncertain manner, still exists. For example, in the 1930s I was told of a Cardiganshire man who went out one evening to visit a friend. He was walking up a narrow lane in the dark silence of the night when suddenly his feet were so 'caught' that he could walk neither forward nor backward. In the darkness he could hear spirit voices and a low murmuring. When this ceased, his feet were released and he managed to turn for home. When he arrived there (said his widow later) he was bathed in sweat and his face had the stamp of death. This is my warning, he said, and went to bed, to die three days later. His son-in-law, a successful London business man, related how the funeral followed the same lane. When the bier and the mourners reached the same spot, the bearers' feet were similarly 'caught' and the funeral had to return and reach the cemetery by a much more circuitous route. But no harm came to the bearers. The widow charged my informant not to breathe a word of all this to 'the chapel folk'. The incident is related here because I have never come across its like in any of the literature.

Since this book is the story of a personal attitude and reaction to the study of folk life, I may be permitted to relate another tale. My father was a country carpenter and as such was often sought for when a fellow countryman died, to make his coffin. My grandfather too was a carpenter. The workshop was below the bedroom where my father and his eldest brother slept. They were awakened one morning about one o'clock by the sound of their father sawing and planing and using his hammer below. This they could not understand for they had seen him go to bed the previous evening. Soon they slept again after being considerably disturbed by the incident. When they went downstairs at seven o'clock they found a neighbour in the kitchen ordering a coffin for his father who had died suddenly at one o'clock that morning. Many years later, when my father had let my grandfather's house to two widowed ladies who used the bedroom above the workshop (then my father's), they also heard my father hard at work in his shop in the early hours before the call came for a coffin. I can vouch for the truth of these happenings for I heard one of the old ladies complaining bitterly of how she was awakened in the early hours by the noise of carpenter's work—as she thought—in the room below. Of such stuff is the folk lore of death.

When my father completed the making of a coffin, he was careful to place in it, under the swansdown drapery, all the shavings from the boards of which the coffin was made. His reason for this was to make the corpse's final resting-place 'comfortable'. But he was always careful to place all the shavings in the coffin. In Brittany, the same care is taken for there is a belief that unless all the shavings are placed in the coffin, Death will come to collect those left out.

The wake (*gwylnos*) still retains its importance in Wales, though it has become a respectable religious occasion in contrast with some wild orgies in some other countries. But in the Solva district of Pembrokeshire until about the middle of the nineteenth century (so an old friend, the late H. W. Evans of Solva, informed me) the wake showed primitive characteristics of a peculiar type. The corpse—without a coffin—was placed on a bench in the kitchen with its feet to the fire. It was covered with a sheet and a metal plate or bowl on its chest. Each person attending the wake placed a candle on the plate. There was much singing and tale-telling. About midnight, two or three of the company sidled out and climbed the roof to the chimney opening. They then let down a rope and cried *chwerwen gwd*. One of the party at the fireside took the rope-end tying it around the corpse's feet, crying *chwarae'n barod* ('the play ready'). Suddenly the corpse was pulled, feet foremost, up through the chimney and let down as suddenly, when it was replaced on the bench. I have no explanation of this barbaric custom. Other customs have been described in the literature.[1]

The Keltic year began on the 1st November which is still known as *Calan Gaeaf* ('the Kalend of Winter'). In contrast with it we find *Calan Mai* ('the Kalend of May'), an alternative form being *Calan Haf* ('the Kalend of Summer'). These two dates were the pivots of the Welsh year. The two kalends retained their importance in Welsh social life but the introduction of the Christian calendar caused a new orientation of beliefs and practices. Christian festivals, notably Easter and Christmas, attracted pre-Christian customs formerly associated with *Calan Mai* and *Calan Gaeaf*. Notably 12th January (*yr hen Galan*—'the old kalend') and subsequently *Calan Ionor* (1st January) became significant. It is noteworthy that New Year's Day remained in the Welsh countryside, as in Scotland, of far more significance than Christmas Day. Even today, Christmastide is known in Welsh as *tymor y gwyliau* ('the season of the *feasts*') which continued into the new year. Consequently we have relics of customs and beliefs associated originally with the Keltic year, reorganized to fit a Christian calendar which was again changed in 1752. The Christian church adopted those customs which it did not see fit to destroy, sublimating them to its own purposes and when necessary investing them with an added ceremonial. The transmutation was completed in some instances with the introduction, from the seventeenth century onwards, of the more severe Nonconformity

[1] See Trefor M. Owen: op. cit. and T. Gwynn Jones: op. cit.

50. Corn dolly suspended in a Yockleton (Shropshire) farmhouse

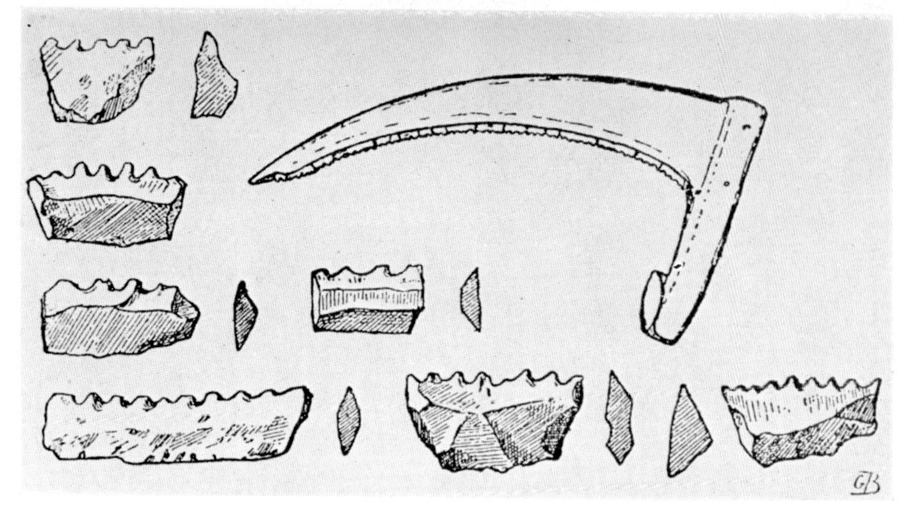

51. Prehistoric sickle, bone, with flint teeth (*after* J. Déchelette: *Manuel d'Archéologie préhistorique*)

52. Sickle, Caernarvonshire, 19th century (in the Welsh Folk Museum)

53. *Car gwyddelig*, Llanharan, Glamorgan (in the Welsh Folk Museum)

54. Slide-car, Glyncorrwg, Glamorgan

55. Wheelcar, Cwmelan, Radnorshire

56. Sled, Llanbryn-Mair, Montgomeryshire. *Photo: G. H. Peate*

57. Gambo, Radnorshire

58. Ox-wain, Ewenni, Glamorgan (in the Welsh Folk Museum)

59. Vale of Glamorgan wagon (in the Welsh Folk Museum)

so that today it is in the preaching and prayer-meeting that we find vestiges of customs which in their origins were far older than the Christian church itself (see, for example, Chapter 7).

Christmas, the Christian festival of the Nativity, 25th December, illustrates well the sublimating influence of the Church. Originally celebrated on various days in December, January and even March, it was fixed by the Western Church in the fifth century on the 25th December, to correspond with the end of the Roman observance of the Saturnalia, and the *natalis invicti solis*, the Mithraic observance of the birth of the Sun. There was much criticism, throughout the centuries, of the Church's decision on the score of idolatry (sun-worship) and as late as the seventeenth century the English Puritans forbade observance of the festival. But the chosen date had wider associations. The Yule feast of northern Europe, a solstice feast to celebrate the lengthening of the day with the return of the sun, and concerned too with the spirits of the dead, became adapted to Christmas, while the Angles, according to Bede, observed the 25th December as their kalend festival. Here then was a classical instance of the Church's adroitness in converting two widely differing pagan feasts—the freedom, indeed license, of the saturnalia and the Yule feast of the dark ancestral spirits—into the prime festival of the Christian tradition.

Accretions to this festival grew throughout the centuries in different countries. In some countries the bestowal of gifts occurred on Christmas Day, in others on New Year's Day. In Wales gifts (*calennig*) were associated with New Year's Day, but the growing anglicization of Wales brought with it the Teutonic custom of the giving of gifts on Christmas Day. The Christmas tree, another German custom, was virtually introduced into Britain by Queen Victoria's German consort: in my native parish I cannot recall ever seeing a Christmas tree during the whole of my childhood: it is certainly a newcomer to Wales. On the other hand, kissing under the mistletoe has a considerable tradition as have the evergreen holly and ivy which remained as decorations until Twelfth Night.

It was at *Calan Gaeaf* (1st November) that bonfires were lit, the period coinciding with the English Guy Fawkes festivities. Guy Fawkes was quite unknown in the Welsh countryside in my boyhood days and it is probable that the fires now associated with him are in reality the survival under a new name of a far older custom. The lighting of the bonfires was attended by various ceremonies which need not be detailed here. When they were burnt out, all would rush home for fear of the *hwch ddu gwta* ('the tail-less black sow'), a fear at one time widespread amongst countrymen. An examination of European folk lore leads one to suppose that primitive man was led to divide his year into two—the beneficent spring and summer and the dark period of autumn and winter. The festivals of the 'dark' period were connected with the belief that at that time certain malign influences had special power. At that time too the souls of the dead were abroad. *Dygwyl y Meirw* ('the feast-day of the dead', All Souls' Day) was of special importance. People went to church to hear spirits call out the names of those who would die during the year: cheese and bread, *bwyd cennad y meirw* ('the food of the messenger of the dead') were distributed among the poor, a custom which can be compared with the gift of soul-cakes.[1]

With New Year's Day, the kalend, was associated the practice of *Calennig*, the collection, principally by children, of new year's gifts. This practice was carried on from the stroke of midnight until noon on New Year's Day. I well remember parties of four or eight young people singing *Y Bwthyn ar y Bryn* and other Victorian airs outside our house about two or three o'clock in the morning and my father, roused from sleep, rewarding them with sixpenny pieces dropped from the bedroom window. Later in the morning, the small children came singing their simple rhymes. The practice ceased at mid-day. In parts of Glamorgan and Monmouthshire, children carried fruit—an apple or an orange—decorated with holly and raisins and studded with grains of oats. Three wooden skewers were fixed into the fruit to form a tripod and a fourth formed a handle. Among the English songs which they sung was the following:

The snow lay on the ground,
The stars shone bright
When Christ our Lord was born
On Christmas night.

[1] See T. M. Owen: op. cit., pp. 136 ff.

'Twas Mary
Daughter of holy Ann
That brought him to this world,
Our Lord made man.

She laid Him on the straw
At Bethlehem,
The ass and oxen shared
The room with them.

In south-west Wales, the *calennig* custom included the sprinkling of water on the hands and faces of the persons called upon. The sprinklers were given money:

Here we bring new water from the well so clear,
For to worship God with, this happy new year;
Sing levy dew, sing levy dew, the water and the wine,
With seven bright gold wires the bugles that do shine;
Sing reign of fair maid, with gold upon her chin
Open you the east door and let the new year in.[1]

Another custom associated with the period between St. Stephen's Day (Boxing Day) and Twelfth Day was that of hunting the wren with due processional ceremony (see Chapter 6). I have dealt with this in detail elsewhere.[2] An echo of the custom is found in the Red Book of Hergest, '*goris Aberriw dryw a drewais*' (below Berriew I struck a wren), and later, in the seventeenth century, Edward Lhuyd gives a description of it in his *Parochialia*. It was formerly the practice throughout Wales to hunt the wren and then carry it in procession in a 'wren house' borne on a bier. It persisted in Pembrokeshire into the 1890s (see Plate 47), but the only traces of it remaining throughout the greater part of Wales are the words of the folk songs associated with it which are found in many districts. The English song found in the Tenby district begins:

[1] E. Laws: *Little England*, 1888, p. 401.
[2] Iorwerth C. Peate: 'The Wren in Welsh Folklore', in *Man*, 1936.

O! where are you going? says Milder to Melder
O! where are you going? says the younger to the elder,
O! I cannot tell you, says Festel to Fose,
We're going to the woods, says John the Red Nose.

This is followed by the question

O! what will you do there? Shoot the Cutty Wren

and in the fifth verse

O! what will you bring her home in?

answered by

On four strong men's shoulders.

This is very similar to most of the Welsh songs. For example:

Ddoi di i'r coed? meddai Dibin wrth Dobin,
Ddoi di i'r coed? meddai Rhisiart wrth Robin,
A ddoi di i'r coed? meddai Siôn wrth y tri,
A ddoi i'r coed? meddai'r cwbwl i gyd.
[Wilt thou come to the wood? said Dibin to Dobin,
Wilt thou come to the wood? said Richard to Robin,
Wilt thou come to the wood? said John to the three,
Wilt thou come to the wood? said all of them.

This is followed by

Beth wnawn ni yno?
[What shall we do there?]

and the answer

Hela'r dryw bach
[Hunt the little wren]

The wren processions included visits to houses, in some cases the sprinkling of water, and monetary rewards.

Reference has already been made (see Chapter 6) to the *Mari Lwyd* which was taken in procession during the 'twelve days of Christmas'. This primitive horse ritual of high antiquity became associated in the peasant mind in post-medieval times with 'holy

Mary' though I tend to the belief that *Mari Lwyd* is more correctly translated as the 'grey mare' with night*mare* attributes. With it was associated the practice of wassailing. In Glamorgan, large-handled pots with ornate lids were produced in the eighteenth and nineteenth centuries, the handles (as many as eighteen in some cases) encircling the belly of the pot. One such wassail bowl (now in the Welsh Folk Museum collection, Plate 49) is dated 'Deber 30, 1834' and bears the maker's name 'Thomas Arthyr'. It is of red earthenware with white slip, characteristic of the products of the Ewenny (Vale of Glamorgan) pottery. This pottery has a long history. Iolo Morganwg states[1] that wassailing took place on Twelfth Night with eighteen-handled bowls (*ffiol ddeunaw ddolennol*). This wassail bowl is an example of the type. The pot and its lid are heavily decorated both with incised zigzags, geometrical and floral patterns and also with applied figures of animals and birds and a complete circle of handles. The apex of the lid has a platform top from which some figures are missing but it is inscribed *Spring* on the one side and *Langan* on the other. These words have nothing to do (as I, for one, once supposed) with either the spring season or the place Llan-gan. The missing figures were those of Tom Winter, nicknamed Spring, who fought a boxing contest at Chichester in 1824 with an Irishman named Langan! The contest lasted one hour and forty-nine minutes and became so well known that, later, Staffordshire jugs depicting the fight were produced and found a ready market. In 1834—ten years after the event!—the Ewenny potters continued the fashion. That a Chichester boxing bout should be commemorated in a Welsh wassail pot ten years after the event is remarkable.

The folk lore of Easter appears to have centred in many countries around the egg. Medieval beliefs that the egg presented an analogy to the mystery of the Resurrection must have influenced folk thought in Christian churches but the use of the egg to celebrate the return of Spring was found in China about 900 B.C. The colouring of eggs at Easter is widespread throughout Europe. In several parts of Wales, children during the week before Easter went around their parish begging eggs. Most of them would collect as many as

[1] G. J. Williams: *Iolo Morganwg*, Cardiff, 1956, p. 40.

two hundred. The china on the dressers of their homes would then be cleared and replaced by the eggs, the eldest child's collection being placed on the top shelf. On their collecting expeditions, they used wooden clappers which were rattled to the accompaniment of a sung phrase or couplet, e.g.

> Clap, clap, os gwelwch chi'n dda ga' i ŵy?
> [Clap, clap, please may I have an egg?]

> Clap, clap, gofyn ŵy,
> Hogyn bychan ar y plwy.
> [Clap, clap, asking for an egg,
> a little boy on the parish.]

The custom persisted in Anglesey at the turn of this century; and indeed still persists although the wooden clappers have now become very infrequent. At one period the custom was fairly widespread in north Wales. It was found in varying forms in other European countries; for example, in Germany a highly decorated figure was carried from house to house by the egg-collectors.

Many summer customs were of particular interest. The festival of May Day (*Calan Mai*—the kalend of May), like Hallowe'en and indeed the Eve of St. John, began on the previous evening. The 'summer birch', or May pole, has already been referred to in Chapter 6, while Owen (op. cit.) has listed a number of customs associated with that period of the year. In Wales, *dydd Sul y blodau* ('the Sunday of flowers') or Palm Sunday has always had a special significance which has persisted to this day in certain districts. As in other countries, the family graves were bedecked with flowers. Willow catkins were used as decorations and were known in some parts of Monmouthshire as 'palms'. They were placed on altars in churches and as decoration in houses.

The 'summer birch' to which I have referred was more characteristic in some districts of Wales of St. John's Eve than of May Day. It is referred to by one of the pre-seventeenth century 'free' verse poets.[1] The celebrated Lewis Morris in the eighteenth century

[1] T. H. Parry-Williams (edit.): *Canu Rhydd Cynnar*, Cardiff, 1932, p. 353.

refers to it as 'the summer pole on the feast-day of St. John' (*dydd gŵyl Ieuan Pawl Haf*):[1] this was in Anglesey. And there are numerous references to the custom in Glamorgan and Carmarthenshire. A blind Glamorgan poet, Wiliam Robert o'r Ydwal, of the eighteenth century, described in verse the 'summer birch' at Wenvoe in the Vale of Glamorgan.[2] The pole was straight and tall: a Sir Edmund Thomas sent carpenters to adze its length and to round it. Then on it were drawn 'pictures' in many colours. The 'maidens' then came and decorated it with many ribbons. On its top was placed a gilded weather-cock with the four quarter signs and around the cock's tails many ribbons and a banner below. It was surrounded by strong able youths to prevent its theft. This last precaution was due to the practice of neighbouring villagers of attempting to steal the pole. A notorious example of such an attempted theft was that in 1768 when the men of St. Nicholas tried to steal St. Fagans's summer birch (see also Chapter 7).[3] Would that 'their painted wooden god' still existed to find a place in the Welsh Folk Museum at St. Fagans! But the custom disappeared completely several generations ago.

The folk lore of the harvest is a varied and rich source of information for the student. Possibly the most interesting feature is concerned with the last sheaf of corn in the harvest itself. Around this folklorists have accumulated a vast amount of theorizing concerning the personification of a harvest spirit in the last sheaf. Into this field of speculation I do not propose to enter. As a general rule the last sheaf of corn in the harvest was left standing uncut. Considerable ceremonial was entered into for its reaping, to which further reference will be made below. It was then taken—with still more ceremonial—into the farmhouse where it was hung to remain until the next harvest. In Gaelic-speaking areas the sheaf was known as the *cailleach* (literally, 'old woman', 'hag') and in some parts of Scotland the *carlin* ('old woman'). In Pembrokeshire, and part of the bordering county of Cardigan, it was known as *y wrach* ('the hag') and in English south Pembrokeshire 'the neck'. The term *gwrach*

[1] Hugh Owen: *The Life and Works of Lewis Morris*, Anglesey Antiq. Soc., 1951, p. 145.

[2] G. J. Williams, in *Llên Cymru*, 1954, pp. 47–50.

[3] *Gwerin*, I, p. 101.

was also known in Caernarvonshire. In the greater part of Wales, however, the name was *caseg fedi* ('harvest mare') or *caseg ben fedi* ('end-of-the-harvest mare'). In England, the sheaf was known as a 'corn maiden', 'corn doll', 'harvest doll', 'kern baby' or 'harvest queen': in Brittany, the Mother sheaf, in Germany, *kornmutter* ('corn mother'), Harvest Mother or Old Woman and even Grandmother; in Denmark, Rye Woman, Old Barley Woman, etc.; in Poland *Baba* or Grandmother. In German, French and Slavonic communities, a wolf was believed to sit in the last sheaf, hence *kornwolf* and the wagon carrying the last harvest load was called the Wolf.[1] In Silesia the last sheaf was known as the *bullkater* ('tomcat').

It is obvious that the concept of the last sheaf as a female person (old woman, hag, mother, grandmother, maiden, queen, baby etc.) was fairly widespread; as an animal (mare, wolf, tomcat), the areas were more restricted. This may have been due to or be responsible for its final shape after cutting, to which we must now turn. The ceremony of *cutting* the last sheaf and of its subsequent handling seems to have been universally similar although there were certain local variations. The custom in Wales was for the headservant to kneel in front of the upstanding last sheaf and, dividing the sheaf into three parts, to plait them together skilfully, securing them below the ears, the tuft, when plaited, standing erect. The reapers, six, eight or more, would then stand at a distance of at least ten yards away and in turn would throw their sickles at the sheaf, the sickles travelling horizontally just above ground level. The intention, of course, was to cut the sheaf. If this were not accomplished after each had thrown his sickle, the headservant, the plaiter, would cut the sheaf himself. The sheaf was taken by the successful reaper to the farmhouse where it was hung from a beam in the living room to show that all the corn had been reaped, and where it remained until the beginning of the next harvest when it was destroyed (Plate 50).

The task of taking the plaited sheaf to the farmhouse was not an easy one. The household was generally warned of its coming and

[1] M. Leach, (edit.): *Dictionary of Folklore, Mythology and Legend*, New York, 1950, *sv*. 'Kornwolf'.

arranged to make difficult its entry into the house. Any suspected bearer was rough-handled by the womenfolk and the plaited sheaf had to be deposited in a *dry* condition on the living-room table. To prevent this the suspected bearer might be drenched with water or any other available liquid. It was only by clever subterfuge that the bearer's battle could be won. When this was attained he was given the place of honour at the harvest feast which followed. In the case of failure the bearer had to sit at the foot of the table, pay a forfeit to the women folk, and be the butt of the evening.

However, there was an alternative to this rough play. The bearer of the sheaf, if he wished, could take it to the field of a neighbouring farm where the harvest had not been completed and throw it in front of the first reaper's sickle. This done, he had to flee for all the reapers would chase him and even throw their hooks at him: if caught he would be bound hand and foot with straw, sometimes so bound, with arms and legs outstretched, on a field gate or thrown into a river or even a cask of pig-feed. A degradation of the custom in Pembrokeshire in 1871–2 was to make a parcel of the sheaf which was then delivered at midnight at the neighbouring head-reaper's house.

The plaiting of the last sheaf was often a fine example of unconscious folk art, particularly in some of the English border counties where in some instances the finished plaiting can be said to resemble a highly conventionalized human figure, a fact certainly related to the names (*gwrach*, *carlin*, *cailleach*, *maiden* etc.) given to it. In countries where it was known as a 'wolf', it is said that the sheaf was plaited to resemble that animal. But I have not seen any instance of a conventionalized 'mare', although it could be argued that some of the Welsh plaited examples were executed in much the same manner as the plaiting of a mare's tail.

One of the much neglected sources of folk lore and custom is what may be generally termed folk literature. This can be well illustrated by reference to the folk verse of south-eastern Wales. *Mesur gwŷr Deheubarth* ('the measure of the men of Deheubarth' [=south Wales])in the form of the *triban* (pl. *tribannau*) was known in the seventeenth century and probably earlier, since it is derived from the classical Welsh metres. It is referred to in a manuscript written about 1716–18. Later it became closely associated with Glamorgan, due to the fertile mind of Iolo Morganwg. In Glamorgan it became a popular medium of folk expression. The stanzas composed in this medium 'have the real merit of presenting to our minds an unsophisticated picture of pastoral life in Glamorgan before the advent of the modern system of farming. They are redolent of the soil from whence they sprang and have in them the very flavour of the life and manners of the period they belong to'.[1] The interested student should compare these quatrains with those of Portugal,[2] for the popular quatrain is a widely-distributed form of folk expression. Many of them were composed and sung by the ploughman who led and followed their oxen. 'There was a set measure and tune to the driver's song which . . . the ox loved, with strains gentle and soothing, and a prolonged note or two in each cadence . . . The words also must be such as pleased his intelligence. A sense of humour had the ox, it must be gratified by some playful nonsense. He was wise, therefore words of sound sense must now and then be chanted to him. He had lively sympathy with those who owned and tended him, therefore the driver could confide to him the story of his love affairs or his varied experiences in service . . . [The quatrains] are the last draught of the exhausted spring of poetry that once flowed side by side with the life of the people.'[3]

These verses lose much in translation if only because of the loss of the verse form with its internal rhyme. Nor can the rich dialect of the Vale of Glamorgan be translated. Iolo Morganwg's translation of one of these quatrains will give the reader however an idea of the form of these verses:

Three things I cannot relish—
A woman that is peevish,
To meet a parson with no wit,
And Llantwit's broken English.

[1] T. C. Evans (*Cadrawd*): 'The Folklore of Glamorgan', in *Cofnodion Eisteddfod Genedlaethol Aberdâr*, 1885, pp. 186–235.

[2] Rodney Gallop: *Portugal*, Cambridge, 1936, chap. X.

[3] Cadrawd: op. cit., p. 188.

The driver praises his oxen:

Dau ych yw Silc a Sowin
Un coch a'r llall yn felyn.
Pan yn aredig yn eu chwys
Hwy doran' gŵys i'r blewyn.

Mae genny' wech bustechyn
Eu gwell ni ellir erfyn;
Hwy dorran' gŵys fu 'rio'd i bath
Am ganllath fel y cordyn.

[Silk and Sowin are two oxen, one red and one yellow.
When they plough in their sweat, they cut a furrow
to a hair's breadth.
I have six oxen: their better cannot be wished;
they plough a furrow the like of which there never was,
for a hundred yards as straight as a cord].

The country boy's fears:

Mae sôn am wrach y rhibyn,
Y tylwyth teg a'r goblin,
A sôn am ysbryd Ladi wen
'N dychrynu plwy Penderyn.

[There is talk of the Evil Eyed Hag, the fairy folk
and the goblin and the talk of the spirit of the
White Lady terrifies the parish of Penderyn.]

A personal nightmare:

Neithiwr mi freuddwydias
Fy mod i'n Sain Nicolas
Gyda'r ffeirad sef Wil Twm
Yn clymu clwm priodas.

[Last night I dreamt that I was in St. Nicholas
with the parson Wil Tom tying the marriage knot.]

Social fears:

O rhyfedd faint y twrw
Sy' i'w glywad drwy Gwmgarw—
Iefan Tomos yn dweud fod glo
I ddod i ma's ohono.

[O, strange the rumours to be heard throughout the Garw Valley—Evan Thomas says that coal is to come out of it.]

The choice of women:

Dywedir ers peth oesa
Taw buwch o'r Fro yw'r gora,
Ond cyn bodloni'r cyflawn serch
Rhaid yw cael merch o'r Blaena.

[It has been said for ages that a cow from the Vale is best, but to satisfy love fully, one must have a *girl* from the Valleys.]

The countryman's love:

Gwaetha'r gwynt yw chwythu,
Gwaetha'r glaw yw gwlychu,
Gwaetha'r dydd yw dod i ben
A gwaetha Gwen fydd pallu.

[The worst of the wind is to blow, the worst of rain is to wet, the worst of the day is that it ends and Gwen's worst is to refuse.]

The countryman's food:

Mi gefas gawl i gino,
Caf gawl i swper heno;
Fe gaiff y feistres fynd i ddiawl
cyn yfa'i i chawl hi eto.

[I had broth for dinner and I shall have broth for supper; the mistress can go to the devil before I drink her broth again.]

Tri pheth ni alla' i aros
Yw enwyn tri phythefnos,
Bara haidd yn llawn o fran
A menyn Siwan Tomos.

[Three things I cannot abide, buttermilk six weeks old, barley bread full of bran and Joan Thomas's butter.]

The countryman's philosophy:

Tri pheth sy'n anodd i nabod—
Dyn, derwen a diwrnod;
Y dydd yn hir, y pren yn gau
A'r dyn yn ddau wynebog.

Gwell bara haidd a heddwch
Na bara can a garwch;
Gwell na llys brenin, Duw a'i gŵyr
Cwrr perth mewn llwyr lonyddwch.

[Three things are difficult to know—a man, an oak tree and a day. Long the day, hollow the tree and two-faced the man.

Better barley bread and peace than white bread and discord; better than a king's court, God knows, a hedge-bank in utter stillness.]

These are simple verses representing only a small corner of the oral tradition of a nation. They serve to emphasize the importance of oral tradition in the field of folk life generally, and for folk lore in particular. Belief survives in the human mind for generations and indeed for centuries, long after the written word has demolished its bases.

Chapter 9

The Countryside

Though many of us stress quite correctly the truth that the student of folk life is concerned equally with town and country, it must not be forgotten that man's most ancient traditions in these islands originated in the countryside—a countryside cultivated by him and in which there grew in the course of time both villages and towns. 'The village' wrote Lewis Mumford,[1] 'multiplied and spread over the entire earth more rapidly and more effectively than the city, and though it is now on the verge of being overwhelmed by urbanization, it maintained the ancient folkways for thousands of years and survived the continued rise and destruction of its bigger, richer, and more alluring rivals.'

Man's life in the countryside is, therefore, of fundamental significance in the study of folk life. There his principal activity has always been agriculture and the various crafts associated, directly or indirectly, with it in village and town. 'Agriculture creates a balance between wild nature and man's social needs. It restores deliberately what man subtracts from the earth; while the ploughed field, the trim orchard, the serried vineyard, the vegetables, the grains, the flowers are all examples of disciplined purpose orderly growth and beautiful form.'[2] Nor can we forget the pastoral side of agriculture, the tending of sheep, the herding of cattle, the breeding of horses—all activities with a profound influence on human communities and on philosophical thought throughout the centuries. In Wales as in some other countries shepherding produced thinkers and poets, while some of its herdsmen and drovers were also among its finest hymn-writers and poets. Readers of George Ewart Evans's

[1] Lewis Mumford: *The City in History*, London, 1961, p. 28.

[2] ibid., p. 450.

sympathetic studies of country life in East Anglia will have appreciated the vast influence of the horse throughout Europe from prehistoric times to the twentieth century.

The processes of pastoralism and of agriculture have formed the bases of man's social development until recent times. Indeed, some of us can still recall the closely-knit compact rural communities in the Welsh uplands; for example, the sheep farmers with their flocks of varying numbers, the sheep-shearing days when all the members of the farming community helped each other in turn, and discussed local and national politics, religion, theology and philosophy at the shearing benches. In due course, each farmer took a part of his wool-harvest to the local woollen mill and to the fuller, there to be converted into flannel and cloth according to family needs, the weaver and the fuller being paid in meat, butter and potatoes. These transactions would be followed in due course by the visit of the tailor to each farm, working for a period of days or weeks in each farmhouse in turn. He, too, would be given lodging and sustenance during his stay and additional payment in kind. The movement of flocks from lowland to upland (and vice versa) had its social complications; for example, the ownership of stray sheep had to be considered and determined, for even the well-established mark of ownership, the sheep earmark, could be tampered with and faked occasionally. This gave rise to another social organization, the 'sheep court' where sheep farmers over a large area and from considerable distances met to assess the evidence concerning stray sheep and related problems and to pronounce a verdict in each case. Despite the often cataclysmic changes in the rural communities of the second half of the twentieth century, several of these courts continue to function on the north-Wales moorlands and probably in other sheep-rearing areas in Britain.

Man, with his mixed diet of flesh and vegetable, found at an early stage in his history that in addition to hunting animals the growing of useful plants and of farinaceous crops was essential. It can be assumed that this revolutionary change in the history of men—the beginning of agriculture—may be said to have first occurred about twelve thousand years ago although no universally precise period can be given where so many societies were, and still are, chronic nomads. But it is certainly true that in western Europe ge the development of agriculture occurred early in prehistori It may be added that the domestication of man himself central factor in the growth of agriculture. Mumford[1] has s that neolithic man's 'concentration on organic life' mean merely a sampling and testing of what nature had provided discriminating selection and preparation, to such good purpose t historic man has not added a plant or animal of major importance to those domesticated or cultivated by neolithic communities'.

Archaeological excavation and research have revealed many traces of prehistoric agriculture, cereals, notably wheat and barley, early sickles, instruments for grinding corn and for breaking and cultivating the ground and also traces of actual fields cultivated. So much theorising, however, has been published in the name of fact concerning 'Keltic fields' and the agricultural implements associated with them that the reader should consult Mr. Ffransis G. Payne's classic paper on 'The Plough in Ancient Britain',[2] before reading any archaeological writings on the subject. The subject is beyond the scope of this book as indeed is the history of agriculture. But mention may be made of some implements.

Let us consider the sickle. Its purpose was to reap and in western Europe examples of this implement from prehistoric times, in bronze and in iron, are plentiful. The metal blade was short—from two and a half to eight inches—in early times, and in form they were hook-like, which may explain why the term 'hook' has persisted to this day for varying types of this implement. The early form of the sickle found, for example, in Egypt (twelfth–eighteenth dynasties), consisted of the jaw-bone of an ox with serrated flint 'blades' inserted in it (Plate 51). Flint sickles were also known in Europe and in Britain. The iron sickles made locally by blacksmiths and used down to the end of the nineteenth century in some localities in Britain were direct descendants of the flint sickle (Plate 52). They were of lunate shape, as were the jaw-bone sickles, with the cutting edge finely serrated, and ending in a fine point. The Industrial Revolution and, subsequently, the development and

[1] ibid., p. 12.

[2] *Archaeological Journal*, CIV, 1948, pp. 52–111.

[illegible]h of machines ended the universal use of such simple implements although, where conditions are unfavourable to the use of developed machinery—on the steep slopes of the Welsh Uplands for example—the hook and the scythe have persisted to this day.

The influence of topography on the tools of agriculture is well illustrated by the history of sleds, carts and waggons. I well remember travelling along one of Glamorgan's busy highways to the village of Llanharan and its coal mine. Climbing from the highway to a farmhouse on the steep slope which rose from the highway I discovered a two-wheeled vehicle, then still in use for harvesting hay and fern. This was typologically a descendant of the still more primitive slide-car. The pair of wheels made for ease of movement on the lower fields of the farm. But the back of the cart was fitted—in the manner of a sled—with a high 'cratch' on which was fitted a windlass type of roller (Plate 53).

Continuing my journey still further I came to the mining village of Glyncorrwg and beyond it to the upland farm of Blaencorrwg (lit. the head of the Corrwg valley). Here I discovered in use the primitive slide-car itself, two poles, joined together by cross pieces in its lower half, the back fitted with a high cratch, each side having a supporting rail and a low movable cratch in front (Plate 54). A horse was harnessed between the top halves of the main poles, the ends of which slid along the ground and the load could be roped tightly with the front cratch pulled tightly against it—the same adjustment that one found in the more developed wheeled example at Llanharan. It is tempting to trace the origin of these vehicles to the hand-barrow (two long poles joined together by cross-pieces) carried by two persons, one at each end, with the load between them. Indeed such a 'barrow' had become a bier in the Oviken mountains, Jämtland, Sweden, and was drawn by one horse, the rear ends of the poles sliding along the ground. In two Merioneth churches there are examples of similar biers but in each case two horses were harnessed, one at each end.

In the industrial area of Glamorgan, therefore, were examples of modern motor vehicles, the wheeled 'slide-car' and the primitive slide-car, all within a few miles of each other and each type surviving because, for its particular purpose, in the restricted area in which it was used, it was the most efficient vehicle for its purpose. The slide-cars were not romantic 'survivals': they co-existed with the modern tractors on neighbouring farms, because they were still the most efficient vehicles on the very steep slopes where they were used.

If lucky, one may still see in travelling along the main roads from Montgomeryshire into Radnorshire, a most cumbersome, indeed ungainly, vehicle crossing the road—but ungainly only on a tar-macadam road. This is the 'wheelcar' (Plate 55) that I once photographed in the Elan Valley. It is, in one sense, a cross between the sled (Plate 56) and the gambo (Plate 57). On modern roads it is useless, for its body consists of two long heavy timbers which are deepest in width in front and there shod with iron strakes. The vehicle has such four corner posts and two cratches inside the wheel that you find in an ordinary hay cart or gambo. The wheels, too, are of gambo type, tyred or straked with iron according to the locality. But the body of the vehicle is *underslung*, *i.e.* the axle tree is above (and not below) the body. When the wheelcar is used on the wet moorland for harvesting peat or heather or even fern on the slopes, the wheels may tend to sink in boggy areas but the wheelcar can slide along without a cross axletree to impede it, the weight of the body being in front.

In the lowlands of Wales, such as the rich Vale of Clwyd in the north and the Vale of Glamorgan, the 'garden of Wales' in the south, draught oxen were used down to the end of the nineteenth century. Folk quatrains extolling these patient beasts were numerous (see Chapter 8). One summer's afternoon in the 1930s a friend took me to Wallas Farm, Ewenni, in the Vale of Glamorgan, to see the farmer and his family. After partaking of a delicious Vale tea, we strolled around the farmyard and entered a barn. There the bay was almost empty awaiting the new supply of hay. In the ruins of the old rick I noticed strange timbering projecting through the remains of the previous year's hay. This, the farmer explained, was the foundation of the hayrick and it had remained there for generations. We removed the covering of hay to discover that the 'foundation' was the body of an ox-wain (Plate 58), in itself a fine piece of folk art. It is a well-known Mediterranean type. The comparatively narrow body has been widened by the addition of broad surboards attached by iron supports to the railed sides, the front and tail being correspondingly wide. The frame is light but strong, constructed of horizontal chamfered rails and ornamental turned vertical balusters, the floor being of boards laid lengthwise. The front and tail are ornamented with wrought iron, the tail-piece including the initials TT, for Thomas Thomas of Cadoxton, near Barry, a well-known eighteenth-century Vale of Glamorgan wheelwright. It was a tragedy that during the time when I was trying to identify this craftsman, all his templates and drawings were destroyed after having been preserved for generations.

The Welsh term for 'wain' is *men* from an earlier *ben* (Gaulish *benna*) (cf. *banne* and *benne* in French: they now have restricted meanings). It is reasonable to suppose that the railed type here is a development of the earlier wicker- or basket-work wagon. William Llŷn (1534/5–1580), a Caernarvonshire poet, describes the ox-wain as 'two golden wheels rolling, by persuasion, along the brow of the valley, a cartwain with grinding sound upon the paved road, the bell that sings the song of the iron hoop. Has it room in front and a place through it to fix the tiller (=ox-pole)? Has it nave and axle and latticed spokes in each wheel?' The body is described as a *cawell* (basket). The poem ends with the splendidly onomatopoeic line

Wich wach yn ôl chwech ychen

(*wich wach*—the 'persuaded' squeak of the wheels—behind six oxen).

Mr. Ffransis Payne in a fascinating Welsh article[1] has discussed the importance of the ox throughout the centuries in Wales and has illustrated in another paper[2] its place from early times in ploughing. The four-wheeled wagon as it was found in Wales was always associated with the horse not the ox and the main types appear to be intrusions from the east into the tongues of lowland along the north and south seaboards and into central Wales. Wagon types have been fully discussed by Mr. J. Geraint Jenkins.[3] But I cannot

[1] 'Cwysau o foliant cyson', in *Y Llenor*, xxvi, 1947, pp. 3–24.

[2] 'The Welsh Plough-team to 1600', in *Studies in Folk Life*, London, 1969, pp. 235–52.

[3] *The English Farm Wagon*, Reading, 1961.

forbear from referring to the Vale of Glamorgan wagon (a development of that of the Vale of Berkeley), one of the most beautiful and satisfying products of Welsh craftsmanship, possessing as Sir Cyril Fox once wrote, 'the seemingly inevitable beauty and fitness of the last phases of the sailing ships and of other specialized creations which have been perfected by generations of men content to work in one tradition'. George Sturt's book *The Wheelwright's Shop* is the classic monument to their craft (Plate 59).

These rural crafts, and many more, were not only part of the life of the countryside but were inextricably woven into the pattern of agricultural life. The country clock-makers, the wood turners, the lip-basket makers (with their simple needle made from a bone from a horse's leg, a segment of a cow's horn the gauge for their coiled straw, and the binding to hold the coils together the peelings from the brambles which the farmer was glad to have destroyed), the love-spoon makers who were farm workers spending their long winter evenings practising their skill with pocket knives, the candle-makers using the rushes from the watery meadows, the carpenters, wheelwrights and coopers, the woollen-mill folk and the tailors—all these and several others were truly agricultural folk. When mechanization and modern transport development overtook the rural communities and when the urbanization of the country village began in recent times, the traditional pattern broke down almost completely, bringing death to the myriad crafts which had survived so successfully for centuries. Where the crafts survived, they suffered considerable change: the village smith became an 'agricultural engineer', often combining with his activities the maintenance of a garage. Most of the small textile mills disappeared and those few which survived became dependent on customers from a wide area far beyond the confines of the local community and latterly on tourist trade. Gone are the days when a farmer could have his clock mechanism made by a local craftsman, its case made from timber grown on his own farm, his kitchen ware made by the local turner, his seedlips and corn containers made by his own servant-men, his rushlights the work of his own women-folk, his furniture, his dairy utensils, his farm implements, his clothes all the work of his neighbours. The ox-wain bearing the proud initials of Thomas

Thomas has given way to vehicles bearing the names of Henry Ford, Ferguson, Massey-Harris and the like. Indeed, the small farm has now too often been pronounced not to be 'viable'.

This metamorphosis has had its effect on the spiritual and cultural life of the countryside. Old values have weakened, the traditional church and chapel going has suffered, the Welsh language has deteriorated and with it the cultural activities based upon it. *Sic transit gloria mundi.*

Chapter 10

Language: a Note

The study of Folk Life can never be complete if one's attention is confined only to material culture. For tradition is the chain which links the present with the past; part of our task is to interpret the life and activity of tradition as a formative and perfective factor in the development of man in society. The principal element in conveying tradition from generation to generation is language, and the study of language is part of folk-life studies. The purpose of an axe is to cut and of a plough to cultivate; on its simplest level, the purpose of language is to communicate. Language is as inherent an element in folk life as are the axe and the plough. Men borrow foreign words into their language as they do implements of foreign manufacture and they assimilate them all into their culture in much the same way. A living language can, therefore, be as much a conglomeration of elements as a piece of machinery in the farmyard.

But throughout the centuries there remain a body of words and a syntactical system which regulates their use and which governs the assimilation of borrowals. These are not inherited but transmitted from father to son; they have to be learnt in just the same way that the young boy has to learn how to use an axe or drive a car, that is, through exercising human faculties in a natural and responsible way. It is in this way that language has developed its finest intricacies such as the Metaphor. Readers of E. B. Tylor will recall his query about the relationship between *junket* and cathedral *canons*. The Greek word κάνυη meant 'a reed or cane' and from it came κανῶν 'measure or rule' and thence *canonicus* 'a clerk under the ecclesiastical rule or canon'. The Latin word for 'reed' was, however, *juncus* which later gave *juncata* 'cream cheese in a *reed*-basket' and so English *junket*. The development of the Greek word for 'reed' gave *canon* and of the Latin word *junket*. Such is the 'mystery' of linguistic development. It is comparable with the development of the steam engine from the steaming kettle.

I have referred to levels of development in material culture—the slide-car, the 'Irish' car, the wheelcar, the gambo, the wagon and the motor lorry, all co-existing to suit their different environments. In the same way, we find the simple speech of the countryman co-existing with the developed vocabularies of the philosophers and scientists. The term 'speech' is used advisedly for as Wartburg has noted:[1] 'It is only through speech that [a language] acquires a real and physically concrete existence . . . Language is a social fact, speech an individual fact'. Indeed, Wartburg has expanded the discussion of 'Language and Speech' in a way that provides us with definitions of value:[2]

'*La langue* is the whole system of expression which serves as a means of communication within a particular human community. It is a system of signs, in which concept and acoustic image come together to form a whole. *It is also a social heritage, and more precisely, it is a set of habits peculiar and common to all the members of a linguistic community.* [The italics are mine.] *La parole*, on the other hand, is the use which each member of the linguistic community makes of this system of expression.'

'Language is also a social heritage.' This is a fact of outstanding importance. Let us consider an instance. The Welsh language belongs to a family of languages of which Breton and Cornish are its sisters and Irish and Gaelic its cousins. While French, Italian and Spanish are languages developed from the Latin speech of the Roman Empire, Latin itself was a member of an older family known as Aryan. Another of the branches of this older family is known as Keltic which was first spoken probably in the upper reaches of the valley of the Danube. Its speakers spread to Galatia in the east and to Italy, Gaul and Spain. We know that by the third century B.C. they were being ousted from these three areas by the might of

[1] Walther von Wartburg: *Problems and Methods in Linguistics* Oxford, 1969, pp. 2, 6.

[2] ibid., Chap. IV.

Rome but traces of their language remain in that area of Europe. The late Professor Henry Lewis[1] has shown that *Eborodunum* (the modern Embrun) in France is the equivalent of Welsh *Dinefwr* (Dynevor), the name elements being in reverse. Similarly, *Lugdunum* (the modern Lyon) compares with the Welsh *Dinlleu*. There are numerous examples of such Gaulish names, and the Gaulish language must have been a descendant of the earlier Keltic. Gaulish too was overcome by Latin and did not survive on the continent of Europe.

But Keltic speakers had crossed the seas and settled in Britain and Ireland and in those islands two branches of this linguistic family survived. These were the Goidelic and Brythonic, the first the parent of the Gaelic of Ireland, Scotland and the Isle of Man, the other of Welsh, Cornish and Breton. By the fifth century A.D. Welsh may be said to have evolved from Brythonic.

This brief historical summary has been necessary since most of the problems of folk life discussed in this volume have been illustrated by Welsh material and the development and survival of the Welsh language present problems of the greatest interest and importance to students of folk life. For Welsh, and before it Brythonic, was once the language of a considerable part of this island but has had gradually to retreat before the inflow of a later language, English, to an area now known as Wales where it was outlawed as an 'official' language by the anglicised royal Tudors over four hundred years ago. Its subsequent survival and development[2] provide a fruitful field of folk-life study.

The population of Wales is approximately two and a half million persons of whom about 650,000 speak Welsh, but only 26,000 persons are monoglot Welsh speakers. Wales, therefore, has English as its official language: out of every hundred of its people, 74 speak English only, 25 speak Welsh and English, 1 speaks Welsh only. In every language census during this century the percentage of Welsh speakers has declined from approximately fifty in 1901 to twenty-six in 1961. This is a situation where the language of a

[1] Henry Lewis: *Datblygiad yr Iaith Gymraeg*, Cardiff, 1931, p. 10.

[2] Iorwerth C. Peate: 'The present state of the Welsh language', in *Lochlann* III, pp. 420–31.

small nation exists as the neighbour of a strong nation speaking a language internationally dominant. The dominant language is 'official', the minority language is not. Here, therefore, is posed a fruitful problem for culture-contact study. This is a problem beyond our present purpose but it may be stated that 'interference'—phonic, grammatical and lexical—in spoken Welsh is becoming increasingly abundant. Indeed, 'new hybrid languages . . . have been formed as a result of the modifications in languages that have been in contact'[1] and this may be almost true of the *Cymraeg Byw* (*lit.* 'living Welsh') which is now being promulgated in certain quarters in Wales. If so, it can only be a transitional stage in the process of murdering an ancient and noble language.

This and its associated problems are matters for the socio-linguistic specialists in the field of folk-life study. 'For two languages in contact, there is a prestige differential, . . . nobody will seriously maintain that it is structural excellence that decides which language community is "upper" and which is "lower". There is often a simple and usable answer to the question: who learns whose language?'[2] Since a policy of bilingualism is being actively encouraged in Wales, the road ahead will lead to a temporary bilingualism ending in a complete English unilingualism.

'A language is inconceivable without the linguistic community which supports it, while the community exists only by virtue of a particular language which shapes and delimits it . . . What sustains a language is, therefore, a community of minds.'[3] Wales is both a linguistic and a national, but a stateless community. It was shorn of its legal system and much else by the Act of Union with England in 1536, leaving only its language as the one bulwark of its nationhood. By the twentieth century, there are thousands of the inhabitants of Wales who consider themselves Welsh but—they have no knowledge of the language nor of the culture and traditions for which it stands. They form no part of the 'community of minds' which has sustained the national personality of Wales throughout

[1] See Uriel Weinreich: *Languages in Contact*, London, 1966, p. 69.

[2] H. M. Hoenigswald: 'Bilingualism, Presumable Bilingualism, and Diachrony', in *Anthropological Linguistics*, 1962, p. 12.

[3] Wartburg: op. cit., pp. 214–15.

the centuries. 'The art of words alone . . . is the appointed utterance of a national culture' and to claim nationality merely on blood and breeding is perilously close to the misbegotten Nazi philosophy. Indeed, there were in Wales as in France poets of the late medieval period for whom the words *language* and *nation* were synonymous, and in the case of Wales it would not be hyperbole to claim that the linguistic community is the nation.

This social significance of language is a basic factor in the development of a folk community. As Jacob Grimm once wrote: 'Whatever your State or your obedience may be, enter into the temple of your ancient and hereditary language whose doors are wide open to you all; learn it and cherish it and hold fast to it, for your strength and survival as a nation depend on it.' This is the sentiment that has inspired the publication in recent years of, for example, a series of vocabularies of technical terms in Welsh in linguistics, metaphysics, aesthetics, music, chemistry, physics and mathematics, wood and metal work, domestic science, physical training, craftsmanship, education, geography, history, biology, the theatre, etc.

All living languages borrow 'for the strength of a vocabulary does not really lie in its "purity"—and purity is in itself a very arbitrary conception when applied to language—but in its adaptability as an instrument'. This is why English *telephone*, French *téléphone*, German, *telephon*, Norwegian *telefon* and the like, become *teléffôn* in Welsh. But the borrowals are formed according to the tradition and rules of the language. The decay sets in when borrowals into the 'minor' language are not assimilated according to its traditional systems, but (whether word or idiom) are transferred bodily from one language to another.

It has been said[1] that the relation of the standard language to dialect—or of language to speech—is illustrated by the myth of Antaeus the giant, son of Gé, the Earth, who was invincible as long as he touched the Earth, his mother. When his enemies were on the point of overcoming him, he would contrive to touch the earth with his body, and the strength of his great mother began at once to pulsate through his veins. In the same way a language retains its

[1] W. J. Gruffydd: 'Yeoman's English', in *Gwerin*, II, pp. 53–7.

vigour as a medium for literature and good writing only by close contact with its dialects, with living traditional speech forms. 'A "dead" language', wrote Gruffydd, 'is not necessarily a language, like Latin or Hebrew, that is no longer spoken; a language may be on the lips of millions of people and yet to all purposes other than the lowest, be as dead as a doornail, which indeed is a very apt comparison since the nail moves with the door, but has no motion of its own.' Loss of contact with dialect has reduced 'Do it please thee to do it?' to the nerveless and dull international slang 'Is that O.K. by you?' This indeed is part of what Gruffydd terms the 'undistinguished *lingua franca*, adequate for the scholar and the scientist, but impossible for the poet and prophet'. In the attempts now being made to evolve a 'basic English' and a 'basic' Welsh for teaching those languages as second languages, there is a serious threat of emasculating each language as a medium of inspired expression by removing from it those characteristics which give it life and vigour. A standard language can be nothing except a form of genteel decay.

The study of living speech is, therefore, an essential duty for the folk-life student. By this means he can accumulate vocabularies relating to craft techniques, to agricultural practices, to domestic pursuits and to all the aspects of a traditional culture. Recording speakers of the oldest generation is an urgent task; with them will disappear a wealth of knowledge and of words. If this wealth disappears from living speech at least it should be preserved in the language archives, from which it may yet prove to inspire and to enrich the literature and the scholarship of future ages.

Bibliography

This bibliography is merely a list of books consulted in the preparation of this volume and which are of interest to students of folk life. Readers should also consult such journals as *Folk Life*, *Gwerin*, *Man* etc. and the bibliographies in many of the works listed below. Of works on specific areas, George Ewart Evans's valuable series on East Anglia (*Ask the Fellows Who Cut the Hay*, *The Horse in the Furrow*, *The Pattern under the Plough*, *Where Beards Wag All*) is outstanding. J. T. Smith and S. R. Jones's survey of Brecknockshire Houses (appearing in parts in *Brycheiniog*, the journal of the Brecknock Society) is an admirable example of how such a survey should be conducted and written up.

1930 ANDERSSON, Otto: *The Bowed Harp*. London.

1899 ANDREWS, William: *Bygone Punishments*. London.

1927 BAILEY, C. T. P.: *Knives and Forks*. London.

1961 BARLEY, Maurice W.: *The English Farmhouse and Cottage*, London.

1952 CUNNINGTON, C. Willett: *English Women's Clothing in the Present Century*. London. See also his series of works on costume.

1969 DARLINGTON, F.R.S., C. D.: *The Evolution of Man and Society*. London. Of outstanding importance.

1957 EDWARDS, Ralph: *A History of the English Chair*. London.

1926 ELLIS, T. P.: *Welsh Tribal Law and Custom in the Middle Ages*. 2 volumes. Oxford.

1937–8 ERIXON, Sigurd: 'Regional European Ethnology'. *Folk-Liv*, I and II, Stockholm.

1942 EVANS, E. Estyn: *Irish Heritage*. Dundalk.

1957 EVANS, E. Estyn: *Irish Folk Ways*. London.

1963 FOSTER, I. Ll. and ALCOCK, L.: *Culture and Environment: essays in honour of Sir Cyril Fox*. London.

1951–4 FOX, Sir Cyril and Lord RAGLAN: *Monmouthshire Houses*. 3 volumes. Cardiff.

1932 GALPIN, F. W. *Old English Instruments of Music.* 3rd Edition. London.
1952 GLOAG, John: *A Short Dictionary of Furniture.* London.
1961 GRANT, I. F.: *Highland Folk Ways.* London.
1965 HYMES, Dell (editor): *Language, Culture and Society.* New York and London. This has lists of works on linguistics.
1961 JENKINS, J. Geraint: *The English Farm Wagon.* Reading.
1965 JENKINS, J. Geraint: *Traditional Country Craftsmen.* London.
1969 JENKINS, J. Geraint: (editor) *Studies in Folk Life: essays in honour of Iorwerth C. Peate.* London.
1930 JONES, T. Gwynn: *Welsh Folklore and Folk Custom.* London.
1967 LAWSON, Joan: *European Folk Dance.* London.
1950 LEACH, M. (editor): *Dictionary of Folklore, Mythology, and Legend.* New York.
1939 LETHABY, W. R.: *Architecture,* 2nd revised edition, London.
1927 LINDSAY, J. Seymour: *Iron and Brass Implements of the English House.* London.
1958 MAXWELL, Stuart and HUTCHINSON, Robin: *Scottish Costume 1550–1850.* London.
1943 MCCLINTOCK, H. F.: *Old Irish and Highland Dress.* Dundalk.
1880 MITCHELL, Arthur: *The Past in the Present.* Edinburgh.
1944 MUMFORD, Lewis: *The Condition of Man.* London.
1946 MUMFORD, Lewis: *Technics and Civilization.* London.
1961 MUMFORD, Lewis: *The City in History.* London.
1967 MUMFORD, Lewis: *The Myth of the Machine.* London.
1971 MUMFORD, Lewis: *The Pentagon of Power,* London.
1873 O'CURRY, E.: *On the Manners and Customs of the Ancient Irish.* London.
1968 OWEN, Trefor M.: *Welsh Folk Customs.* 2nd Edition. Cardiff.
1948 PAYNE, Ffransis G.: 'The Plough in Ancient Britain'. *Archaeological Journal.* CIV.
1964 PAYNE, Ffransis G.: *Welsh Peasant Costume.* Cardiff.
1929 PEATE, Iorwerth C.: *Guide to . . . Welsh Bygones.* Cardiff.
1930 PEATE, Iorwerth C.: 'Welsh Piggins'. *The Connoisseur.*
1936 PEATE, Iorwerth C.: 'The Wren in Welsh folklore'. *Man.*

1941 PEATE, Iorwerth C.: 'The Place of folk culture in the museum'. *Museums Journal*, 41.

1942 PEATE, Iorwerth C.: 'The double-ended firedog'. *Antiquity*.

1943 PEATE, Iorwerth C.: 'The Pot-oven in Wales'. *Man*.

1946 PEATE, Iorwerth C.: *The Welsh House*. 3rd edition. Liverpool.

1963 PEATE, Iorwerth C.: 'Mari Lwyd—Láir Bhán'. *Folk Life* I.

1971 PEATE, Iorwerth C.: 'Corn Ornaments'. *Folklore*.

1964 RAGLAN, Lord: *The Temple and the House*. London.

1901 RHŶS, Sir John: *Celtic Folklore*. 2 vols. Oxford.

1965 RIMMER, Joan: 'The Morphology of the triple harp'. *Galpin Society Journal* XVIII.

1952 SALZMAN, L. F.: *Building in England down to 1540*. Oxford.

1933 SAYCE, R. U.: *Primitive Arts and Crafts*, Cambridge.

1963 SMITH, J. T.: 'The Long-house in Monmouthshire: a re-appraisal'. *Culture and Environment*, London.

1964 SMITH, J. T.: 'Cruck Construction: a survey of the problems'. *Medieval Archaeology*, 8.

1969 SMITH, J. T.: 'The Concept of Diffusion in its application to vernacular building'. *Studies in Folk Life*, London.

1936 THOMPSON, A. Hamilton: *The English House*. London.

1929 TYLOR, E. B.: *Primitive Culture*. 2 vols. London.

1935 WILLIAMS, Iolo A.: *English Folk-Song and Dance*. London.

1956 WILLIAMS, Griffith John: 'Glamorgan customs in the eighteenth century'. *Gwerin*, 1.

Index

Index